D1557620

Heidegger and the Politics of Poetry

Heidegger and the Politics of Poetry

PHILIPPE LACOUE-LABARTHE

❦ ❦ ❦

Translated and
with an Introduction by Jeff Fort

University of Illinois Press
Urbana and Chicago

Ouvrage publié avec le concours du Ministère français
chargé de la culture—Centre National du Livre.

The publisher gratefully acknowledges that this work is published with
the assistance of the French Ministry of Culture—the National Centre
of the Book.

Originally published as *Heidegger, La Politique du poème,*
by Philippe Lacoue-Labarthe. Copyright © Éditions Galilée, 2002.
Translation and introduction © 2007 by the Board of Trustees
of the University of Illinois
Manufactured in the United States of America
C 5 4 3 2 1

∞ This book is printed on acid-free paper.

Library of Congress Cataloging-in-Publication Data
Lacoue-Labarthe, Philippe.
[Heidegger. English]
Heidegger and the politics of poetry / Philippe Lacoue-Labarthe;
translated and with an introduction by Jeff Fort.
p.   cm.
Includes bibliographical references (p.) and index.
ISBN-13: 978-0-252-03153-3 (cloth : alk. paper)
ISBN-10: 0-252-03153-9 (cloth : alk. paper)
1. Heidegger, Martin, 1889–1976. 2. Poetry. I. Title.
B3279.H49L25313   2007
193—dc22   2006022579

❦ ❦ ❦　To the memory of Roger Laporte,
writer and friend

Contents

Translator's Introduction:
The Courage of Thought

One of Martin Heidegger's late lectures from the 1960s bears the title "The End of Philosophy and the Task of Thinking."[1] In it he asks what task might remain for thinking in the age of philosophy's completion and its dispersion in the techno-sciences. His insistence that the task of thinking must be pursued outside a henceforth untenable philosophical determination is only the continuation of concerns that go back at least three decades earlier, when the site of this other task of thinking was first made explicit: In the 1930s Heidegger had very clearly laid this task at the feet of poetry, or rather of a particular poet, in the extensive and detailed readings that would be devoted to Hölderlin, whose "thinking poetry" would open the way to a new beginning (we will see in a moment what Heidegger thought should be begun anew). But in doing so, Heidegger not only assigned to poetry the task of a thinking that philosophy could no longer accomplish, he also attempted to weigh it down with a historical "mission" dictated, it must be said, by a political program based on *a mytho-poetic annunciation of the historical destiny of Germany and the German people.* The perfectly legible and explicit articulation of this program in Heidegger's discourse on Hölderlin—that is, the central place of this program in Heidegger's *thought*—is the scandal, and the predicament, at the heart of the lectures by Philippe Lacoue-Labarthe collected here.

The context in which Heidegger undertook to read Hölderlin is of course far from indifferent. Initiated in 1934, just after the infamous and aborted episode of the Rectorship of Freiburg University, these readings were carried out almost in their entirety under the Third Reich and during the war;[2] they represent both a withdrawal from the overt political engagement and an extension of this engagement's *topoi* into another sphere: poetry as politics carried on by other means. For in differentiating himself from the Nazis, Heidegger remains no less of a nationalist, only a more "thinking" one. . . . To be sure, he does differentiate himself—and Lacoue-Labarthe insists that we recognize this—both in the readings of Hölderlin and, especially, in the lectures on Nietzsche from the same period, in which he speaks repeatedly against the "biologism" imputed to the latter. Put somewhat crudely, it could be said that in response to the Nazi pathos around "Blut und Boden," although Heidegger rejects blood, his feet remain firmly on the soil for which the Nazis fought. And that is precisely what is at stake throughout his readings of Hölderlin, in which no motif is more insistent than that of the *Heimat* and the home: however inflected by strangeness, homelessness, and the uncanny (*Heimatlosigkeit, Unheimlichkeit*) this motif may be, no matter how "essentially" it is articulated, the destiny at issue remains specifically *located*.

This becomes clearer than ever if, without reducing Heidegger's thought to a mere effect of its context, we do insist on reading him in context, particularly with regard to Hölderlin. Not only, then, do we find explicit statements in which the appearance of the signifier "Germany" cannot fail to produce a chill, we see how clearly Heidegger's "sermonizing" (as Lacoue-Labarthe calls it) alludes to the concrete political situation of the day. Consider the truly stunning remarks from the final paragraphs of "*Heimkunft / An die Verwandten*" ("Homecoming / To Kindred Ones"), a lecture addressed to a wartime audience in 1943 and included as the opening piece in his principal collection of writings on Hölderlin, *Erläuterungen zu Hölderins Dichtung* (*Elucidations of Hölderlin's Poetry*). At issue here is the homecoming of the poet, and of those to whom he returns:

> Assuming [. . .] that those who are merely residents on the soil [*Boden*] of the native land are those who have not yet come home to the homeland's very own; and assuming too that it belongs to the *poetizing* essence of homecoming, over and above the merely casual possession of domestic things and one's personal life, to be open to the origin of the joyful; assuming *both* of these things, then are not the sons of the homeland, who, though far distant from its soil, still gaze into the cheerfulness of

the homeland shining toward them, and use up their life and expend it on the path of sacrifice [*ihr Leben . . . verwenden und im Opfergang verschwenden*] for the still reserved find [*gesparten Fund*]—are not these sons of the homeland the poet's closest kin [*Verwandten*]? Their sacrifice shelters within itself the poetic call to what is most dear in the homeland, so that the reserved find may remain reserved.[3]

To be sure, this passage comes at the end of lengthy developments that give many of its terms a density and signification not conveyed by quoting the paragraph in isolation, and in any case there are many elements that would require commentary. (What is the "reserved find"? who exactly are the "sons of the homeland"? how is this "verwenden" turned toward the "Verwandten"?) It is important to insist that Heidegger's readings always accrue an irreducible richness, complexity, and ambiguity. And yet the crude and glaring reference remains: Who in Germany in 1943 would not hear this talk of the "sons of the homeland . . . far distant from its soil" *also* as a reference to the soldiers fighting and dying, at that very moment—and thus (in the logic of the slippage that occurs here) sacrificing themselves for the poetic "homecoming" of Germany to itself? In this they are akin to the great poet himself; they are carrying out the same sacred mission. In the next paragraph, Heidegger completes the thought: "This homecoming [*Heimkunft*] is the future [*Zukunft*] of the historical essence of the Germans." Poet and soldier fighting on the same national-spiritual front? Allied, or closely akin, across their different functions, in this most difficult but promising futurity? Elsewhere Heidegger speaks of the poet as "the first sacrifice" in uncovering the "foundational ground [*Stiftungsgrund*]" for the "destiny of Germany's future history."[4]

Such quotations show Heidegger at his worst, in a way that can be considered *topical:* they engage his place (and time). But in this light the political thrust of Heidegger's *use* of Hölderlin is so manifest, blatant, and unabashed that, today, it is astonishing that anyone could read the *Elucidations,* in particular, without this aspect emerging as *the* salient feature of this project—simultaneously its most distant (longed-for) horizon and its very center of gravity. Again, such a response is not based on any reductionism, nor should it lead to an unthinking dismissal (on the contrary). But these problems must be registered in their proper proportions and importance; and it must be recognized that whatever is worth retaining from this discourse must first be carefully rescued from its preponderant compromises—assuming this is possible. The days of glibly apolitical readings of Heidegger are, or should be, over. If the so-called "Heidegger affair" that last emerged in the late 1980s (but which, as Lacoue-Labarthe has pointed out, revealed nothing essentially new) had any salutary effect, it has been to force Heidegger's readers to confront his politics as articulated *in his thought*.

Lacoue-Labarthe was already doing that.[5] For his purposes here, he does not need to open the sinister "dossier" detailing Heidegger's tragicomic tryst with party politics, since, as heinous and condemnable as that episode is, and as necessary as it is to register it too in relation to Heidegger's work, it does not engage the essential. Rather, Lacoue-Labarthe simply opens the published work—and reads. One of his primary aims in doing so has been nothing other than to demonstrate not that Heidegger was a Nazi, but that, in his *agon* with the vulgarity of Nazism—by which, Lacoue-Labarthe says, he was merely "disappointed"—Heidegger was, at a much more profound level, the thinker of the essence of National Socialism. And moreover that he is this thinker *especially,* and most explicitly, in his very "politicized" reading of Hölderlin. It is through these demonstrations that Lacoue-Labarthe, no doubt more than anyone else, has sensitized us to these difficulties from within the exigencies of thought itself.

The indictment of Heidegger (and it certainly is one) that Lacoue-Labarthe presents here is thus not limited to a mere condemnation. "I am simply making a statement," he says. And yet the tone here is somewhat harsher than the one heard in *Heidegger, Art, and Politics,* more impatient and less mitigated by gestures of defense, or by hyperbolic praise. (Lacoue-Labarthe has recognized Heidegger as "incontestably the greatest thinker of the age";[6] he says nothing like that here.) The focus is on the blind spots and the *faults* discernible in Heidegger's thought, particularly concerning Hölderlin, on the one hand, and the (Romantic) desire for myth, on the other. This is not a reference to the biographical "myth of Hölderlin": the mad poet whose madness made of poetry a prophetic, if unstable and painful, utterance. There is in fact no trace of this in Heidegger, as one would expect.[7] But if Heidegger did not succumb to the myth of the poet, he did succumb to the temptation, says Lacoue-Labarthe, to mythologize poetry. And he did so on the basis of what is here called (in an extension of analyses developed in earlier writings)[8] Heidegger's "onto-mythology"—an unsavory mixture of unacknowledged cultural-historical tendencies (inherited particularly from Romanticism) and disavowed religious longings (disavowed with regard to the word, if not in fact). Any discourse that prides itself on being largely evacuated of any unreserved affective investments (one might say, of all "hope") is bound to be highly revealing in those places where its pathos shows through; in a discourse as deeply and massively critical of the tradition as Heidegger's, this pathos is likely to take the form of submission. That is very much the case with the reading of Hölderlin: It submits itself entirely to the authority of the text it reads (or—in an important complication—to the authority it *confers* on this text), such that, in a well-known phrase from Paul de Man, "Hölderlin is the only one whom Heidegger cites as a believer cites Holy Writ."[9] The extraordinarily exalted privilege accorded to the poet by the thinker cannot but indicate the depth of investment in the project in which the poet has been enlisted—or for which he has been "elected," to use Heidegger's term. Likewise, it points toward an occultation of what essentially sets this investment in motion. The unthought of Heidegger's (nationalist) thinking is to be found, at least in part, in the legacy that Romanticism left in Germany (that is, in the mimetic aporias of its longing for, and rivalry with, the grandeur of the Greek beginning).[10] And in the wake of this legacy, Heidegger's "election" of Hölderlin has been a dubious honor, not to say a burden. By elevating the poet's position to the point of making Hölderlin (as Lacoue-Labarthe has written) "purely and simply what is at stake in thinking itself,"[11] by laying out the problematic within a fundamentally mythic structure, and by providing a reading of Hölderlin that, in fact, in its depth of resources and detailed elaboration, has become an inevitability in any confrontation with the poet, Heidegger has, as it were, internally colonized the text of Hölderlin. It is as though one aspect of this text had been forced to subjugate, or even to eject, another incompatible one. This situation is the source of one of the imperatives that Lacoue-Labarthe formulates and responds to here: to delineate and make heard another Hölderlin, one who not only "paralyzed in advance" the theological-political program that Heidegger wants him to have founded, but who himself articulates a very different poetic task—and thought—moving precisely in the opposite direction.

⚜ ⚜ ⚜   Through a "friendly debate" with Alain Badiou on the relationship between poetry, philosophy, and politics, Lacoue-Labarthe reaffirms that element of the Heideggerian approach to poetry that, he believes, deserves to be pursued: that there is a "task of thinking" proper to poetry, and that this task does involve a strategic and even a "calculated" historical inscription. Like Badiou, who speaks of "unsuturing" poetry from philosophy, Lacoue-Labarthe wants both to critique—to undo—the philosophical capture of poetry and thus to release poetry into another mode of language (which he calls "prose"), another incision of history into poetry, and vice versa. But unlike Badiou, he does not want to do this for the sake of reestablishing philosophy on its original (Platonic) basis. Rather, he turns to other very different allies, namely Benjamin and Adorno, whom he places alongside Heidegger, and in relation to Hölderlin, not simply to provide a contrast, but to establish a differend on the basis of a strange complicity in which their preoccupations converge. This complicity involves, above all (to put it succinctly), the recognition of an imperative specific to the poetic task, and of the abyssal necessity for a thought of the proper. It is not surprising that Lacoue-Labarthe would discern this complicity, for he shares it. And it is clear that in this differend he has taken sides.

Benjamin's remarkable essay, "Two Poems by Friedrich Hölderlin," predates Heidegger's readings by almost twenty years and is in any case separated from them by a chasm of multiple differences. And yet there is an uncanny resonance in the language used by each of them, particularly in the term that most punctually marks their common terrain and its unexpected point of contact: *das Gedichtete.* "The poetized" or, as Lacoue-Labarthe prefers, "the *dictamen.*" However diversely this term may be used in the authors in question here, it means at least this (to put it in simple terms): that element of a poem that the poem *had to say* so that it might be attested to; it is thus, in a sense, the poem's attestation of its own origin and conditions of being. The question is whether such a saying is a "mything" (as Heidegger insists, somewhat covertly, through his use of the term *Sage*), or whether it is, rather, *resolutely prosaic*. Such a notion raises a number of important issues, but here, too, Lacoue-Labarthe makes it clear what decision he has made regarding this question.

The prosaism called upon here is intimately bound up with the earthward trajectory of "Hölderlin's itinerary" (as Blanchot called it),[12] as well as that of Rimbaud (who emerged from the otherworldly hell of poetry only to recede into the desert). But in relation to the poetic task it determines, it is not without a certain "transcendental" dimension. Echoing the Kantian language used by Benjamin throughout his essay, Lacoue-Labarthe finds there an indication, at least, of nothing less than the "transcendental schema of poetry." According to this rich suggestion, the poem would be "schematized"—it would enter into the order of phenomena—driven by an imperative to bear witness to the "life" and the "world" (in Benjamin's terms) that give rise to the imperative itself (this is its essentially reflexive structure). And this very originary experience requires courage, "the courage of (or for) poetry." But if such a formulation attempts to transcribe the Kantian schematism into the sphere of poetic activity (in the broadest sense) and, simultaneously, into the language of an imperative, it does so in the mode of a constitutive failure already legible in the imperative itself: *il faut* (it is necessary). Lacoue-Labarthe's reading of this French phrase as a command already inhabited and riven by a *fault* that twists it, necessarily, in the direction of its own failure—into a command also to fail—resonates felicitously with the English terms called for here (derived from the same Latin roots). Indeed, it recalls an anglophone writer, mentioned briefly in this book's central essay, who expressed the injunction in these very terms: "Fail again. Fail Better," writes Beckett in *Worstward Ho* (a text invaded by grammatical imperatives), conjoining failure, repetition, and "the good" in a strange ethics of impossibility not far removed, in fact, from the linguistic schematism hinted at in Lacoue-Labarthe's formulation.

What Benjamin in his essay on Hölderlin calls "life" (or "world"), placing it in close proximity with the courage to undergo an intransitive imperative, Lacoue-Labarthe has elsewhere called "experience."[13] The word itself immediately evokes the necessity for courage; derived from the Latin *experiri*, it means the traversal of a danger or peril (*periculum*), a test, trial, proof, or ordeal. In French: *épreuve*. Referring to the very "singular idiom" of Paul Celan, Lacoue-Labarthe asks whether a singular experience can be written, or whether language does not destroy singularity from the beginning, either by dispersing it into "meaning" or by enclosing it within an inaccessible private code. Between these two traps—dangerous or inconsequential—poetry addresses itself to the Other, that is, it inscribes itself into history at the very edge of the sayable. And it does so in, through, and as an imperative (a *dictamen*). In this sense, the schematism of poetry is the point at which experience *must be written,* precisely there where it falters. In other words: transcendence is (an) imperative—but in default. The linguistic dimension of this experience is what points us toward the archi-ethical dimension of modern poetry as Lacoue-Labarthe conceives it.

The "negative" or critical aspect of this book is thus accompanied by a direct engagement with the very matter and possibility of poetry as it stands at present, a decisive (but open-ended) statement about what poetry can or ought to be, its responsibilities, its foreclosed or tired reflexes, its pitfalls and risks. What are the chances and futures of poetry today? What kind of poetry ought to be possible now, and what kind ought not to be (even if it is produced in profusion)? In Lacoue-Labarthe's thinking, a certain privilege is given to the lyric; that is the "genre" of Hölderlin's greatest achievements, and Celan's. It is also the most modern mode of poetry, though it is no doubt burdened by that most modern of problems: the subject. Lyric poetry may of necessity be a "subjective" poetry *in some sense,* but it need not be a subjectivist indulgence. In an interview from 1987, Lacoue-Labarthe points to a "subjectivist retreat" in contemporary poetry, saying (in a deliberately abrupt formulation): "If the question we are confronted with has to do with *saying nothing,* having nothing to say is no response, and to 'encrypt' this nothing, that is, to privatize it, even less so." The important thing, he adds, is to confront "what *it is necessary* to say, of which, strictly speaking, we know nothing."[14]

Far from any mythologizing reinvigoration, and in a mode that cannot be considered as simply "handing philosophy over" to poetry

(Badiou), what Lacoue-Labarthe seeks is that point where poetry and thought each emerge in the very risk of an unknowing imperative, in the experience—the acknowledgment and articulation—of a historical destitution that makes no promises of any kind. Any poetry that speaks this experience would have to be a thinking poetry—and the schematism would also once again be a schematism of thought, it too requiring courage.

❦ ❦ ❦   In 2000, Lacoue-Labarthe published a book of poetry entitled *Phrase*.[15] I cannot resist concluding here by commenting on it briefly, in a somewhat personal way (and at the risk of being anecdotal, but not *merely*). It contains a poem that bears witness, in fact, to an experience and a place that is clearly marked and identifiable: California, particularly San Francisco and the Bay Area, in the early and mid-1990s (it is dated "1993–3 March 1996"). This is the period when Lacoue-Labarthe gave his last seminars at the University of California at Berkeley (and when I was a graduate student there). The poem is, in part, a kind of "adieu" to that time and place; among its first sentences it reads: "But I won't be going back there again, that's for sure, / and I can see I'll have to get used to the idea / that that was the last time."[16] Punctuated by numerous phrases in English (several from Eliot and Conrad), it evokes the mood of someone who is taken aback, astonished, and disoriented, *dépaysé*, by a strange and calmly hellish foreign place. Toward the end is a section that shows the poem's sunstruck—Hölderlinian—inspiration, and the quiet turbulence of a stubborn but disarmed resistance, this time with reference to the sun of another "West," both starkly clear and deeply unsettling:

> At times the sky is what moves us,
> by being so blank, and lit with such intensity,
> especially in the evening, that in our abandonment, yes,
> the fever leaves us and tears are no help at all.
> But no is the word, no to the unacceptable
>
> calm, no to the dizziness, for this slowness
> before the crossing, as it dies away, there's no doubt
> the suspense is finely calculated, just on the threshold

> of the ultimate declaration that returns from far away
> like an unexpected squall or storm, unexpected, that is,
> were it not for the silence, you know, precisely that silence.
> [...]

✻ ✻ ✻   I would like to thank Bill Regier of the University of Illinois Press for his receptiveness to, support of, and patience with this project. My thanks also go to Ann Smock for her helpful suggestions with the manuscript. I would like to acknowledge the translation of "Le courage de la poésie" by Simon Sparks published in *The Solid Letter*, ed. Aris Fioretos (Stanford, Calif.: Stanford University Press, 1999), which I consulted with profit. Finally, I would like to thank Philippe Lacoue-Labarthe for (among other things) the inspiring seminar he presented at the University of California at Berkeley in 1991, which gave rise to "Il faut"—translated here less out of necessity than out of deep appreciation and gratitude.

Heidegger and the Politics of Poetry

Author's Preface

This book is, strictly speaking, of a *mathematical* order: Made up of texts written and reworked, for the most part, between about 1990 and the past few months, it retraces the history of an "apprenticeship" or the experience of a gradual—and sometimes difficult—understanding. Both of these—the apprenticeship and the experience—came out of earlier work, particularly *La fiction du politique*,[1] and consequently (since my stubbornness is so apparent here) from a tenacious question that is itself at bottom quite painful; so much so that, when Heidegger is in question (and Heidegger will have always been in question, or almost always, in that part of my activity that can be considered "philosophical"), it gravely undermined an admiration that, nevertheless, somehow still remained intact—as though through a strange "schizophrenia" whose origin and persistence have to this day not ceased to trouble me. To say the least.

Initially, the question was this: Whence Heidegger's scandalous political engagement, at the time of Nazism, and *in* Nazism? This question was gradually transformed into another: How is it that, at bottom, a certain idea of History, and consequently of art, provided a more and more explicit authorization and foundation for this engagement? And finally the question came to be formulated thus: Why is Heidegger's interpretation of poetry—if we recognize that for him art is in fact essentially Poem—scandalous to such a degree? And it is immediately clear that this formulation carries these questions beyond the strict boundaries of what is called the "political engagement" (his membership in the Nazi party between 1933 and 1945, if you like), or that at the very least it casts the shadow of these questions over his entire work, up to the very end.

In a certain way, that is all.

But I must say one more thing; otherwise this would, after all, be rather cursory.

The volume as it is presented—as a collection of lectures, essentially—in no way claims to offer an exhaustive treatment of a question that has long been the subject of much discussion: Heidegger and poetry. Nothing will be "covered" here.

On the one hand, my focus in these lectures is primarily Heidegger's commentary on Hölderlin, for many reasons that are not exclusively "philosophical," relating rather to certain other projects in which I have been engaged (translation, theatrical work, etc.).[2] I make very little mention, for example, of Heidegger's reading of Stefan George, nor especially that of Georg Trakl, which has been so rigorously and accurately situated by Jacques Derrida.[3]

On the other hand, I have deliberately omitted from this book the beginnings of a rather "harsh" analysis of some two or three pages on Rimbaud that were extorted from Heidegger late in his career.[4] This is one of the rare places, however (and this cannot fail to be revealing), where Heidegger ever ventured to comment, however furtively, on a text in a language other than Greek or German (or even Latin). This commentary is indeed quite venturesome (as were the writing and publication of certain "poems" or an exchange, in his last years, with René Char), and it requires a very different approach; this analysis will eventually appear, if all goes well, in a separate study.

Finally, although I have ventured to do so once or twice, I will not directly address here the question of "religion" in Heidegger; or rather—since, following a tradition firmly established since the Reformation, Heidegger never accepted the word or the concept of "religion" (judged to be too exclusively "Roman" or "Latin")—the question of the "holiness" to come. Indeed, this latter is elaborated entirely on the basis of the reading of Hölderlin, and it is indissociable from the strangely "political" itinerary that that reading continually follows; but while a contestation of Heidegger's contestation of "religion," according to *all* its political implications, still seems to me to be an indispensable task, it would be impossible to acquit oneself of this task in a few pages, and even less in the form of a postscript.

March 2002

✣ ✣ ✣   Prologue:
           Heidegger's Onto-Mythology

In his 1935 course *Introduction to Metaphysics,* as part of the first commentary he devoted to Sophocles' *Antigone* and the well-known *stasimon* on *technē,* Heidegger considered it necessary to "insert a *remark* in order to ward off a widespread misinterpretation of this entire poem, one that lies close at hand for modern man."[1] Sophocles' poem, he says, is in no way a description of "the various fields of activity" of man, who would appear as "one being among many"; and above all it does not "recount the development of humanity from a wild huntsman and a traveler by dugout canoe to a builder of cities and person of culture."[2] "The fundamental error that underlies such ways of thinking," he then explains, "is the opinion that the inception of history is primitive and backward, clumsy and weak. The opposite is true. The inception is what is most uncanny and the most violent."[3] (And we know that with these two terms—*unheimlich* and *gewaltig*—Heidegger intends to restore the truth of the original meaning of the Greek *deinon,* as it resonates in the chorus of *Antigone: polla ta deina,* etc.).

And here, almost immediately afterward, he inserts the following declaration: "The inexplicability of this inception is no defect, no failure of our knowledge of history. Instead, the authenticity and greatness of historical knowing lie in understanding the character of this inception as a mystery. Knowing a primal history [*Wissen von einer Ur-Geschichte*] is not ferreting out the primitive and collecting bones. It is neither half nor whole natural science, but, if it is anything at all, it is mythology [*Mythologie*]."[4] Given the "dark times" then prevailing, and even considering the relative but undeniable distance that Heidegger had placed between himself and the National Socialist regime by resigning from the rectorship, the luster of such a declaration is itself rather somber. At least for two reasons.

To claim, at the particular moment when Heidegger says this, that the only legitimate "knowledge" of history and its origin is a "mythology," if not *the* mythology—over and against all the sciences, such as paleontology, prehistoric research, ethnology, cultural history, etc., which are presumed to be subservient to the model of the natural sciences—is a gesture that cannot avoid a clear and immediate political echo; or, more rigorously, an aesthetico-political echo. As I have tried to show elsewhere[5]—and this is fully evident in any case—beginning with the initial *envoi* of Romanticism and speculative Idealism (roughly, from 1800 to 1815 and the end of the *Aufklärung*),[6] and under the agonistic compulsion or the mimetic double bind that nearly always makes it impossible for the Modern to extricate itself from the Ancient except by repeating it, the dream of an entire "German ideology" was to invent a myth or to institute a "great art." These were deemed to be the only means capable of bringing a people (a "nation") into its true historical dimension; or, as Heidegger continually repeated in the 1930s and 1940s, the only means capable of *constituting an origin* for a people's "historial Dasein." This dream provided the fundamental underpinnings for the *Kulturkampf* and the anti-Catholic—but not anticlerical—politics of the "Imperial Age" (that of Bismarck). Such a dream was given a laborious illustration by Wagner and a rigorous structure by Nietzsche (who also gave it more than that: it is enough to think of *Thus Spoke Zarathustra* by the so-called "early Nietzsche"), and it is certainly not absent from the National Socialist project. Indeed, it even constitutes that project's solidest and most powerful armature, its least vague and least hastily sketched guideline, the one that delimits it with the greatest precision even into its constitutive anti-Semitism—an anti-Semitism that was presented officially as "scientific" but was in reality aesthetico-ethnic (the Jew as a "caricature"—this is Winckelmann's expression—in opposition to the "athletic body" of the Greeks or the "regenerated" Germans). National Socialism remains incomprehensible if we do not perceive in it an essentially *technical* utopia, in the two senses that today we can make resonate in this word: art and technoscience. It is one of the final results, and the most terrifying by far, of the metaphysics of the Moderns. It is not simply a particularly cruel and systematically deliberate manifestation of state terrorism, of a police "governmentality," of "total mobilization" and social militarization, of "bio-power" or of the despotism inherited from the former empires and the feudal "milieux" (that is, of politico-financial piracy)—or, in an even more banal register, of Capital suddenly overcome with panic. Brecht was not always right; no more than were a number of others who came after him. . . .

It is certainly true that Heidegger had no trouble demarcating himself from most of the "major" ideologues of the modern necessity of myth (beginning with Georges Sorel) and, especially, of the new German myth (Rosenberg, Bäumler, Krieck). It is also true that when it comes to Wagner, or Wagnero-Nietzscheanism, he cannot find harsh enough words; and we know that for almost six years, after the obscene adventure of the rectorship, he was continually at pains to extricate Nietzsche from his fascist interpretation, and, with reference to the most sensitive points (will to power, aestheticism or physiological aesthetics, biologism), to strictly delimit his rightful place in the terminal phase of metaphysics. It is obviously impossible simply to confuse Heidegger's positions with those of Nazism, although such a confusion does seem to have occurred, or at the very least to have made a sketchy appearance, in the phraseology of 1933.

But we must not obscure the matter. Beneath the apophantic rhetoric or the constant denial authorized by (and authorizing) "fundamental ontology"—in the form "my thought on art is not an aesthetics; my reading of Hölderlin has nothing to do with poetology; my interpretation of History owes nothing to any sort of historicism; my statements on the destiny of peoples or on the possibility of Germany's existence do not have the slightest 'political' resonance"—that is, in the end, "my 'philosophy' is not a philosophy" (which in a certain sense is undeniable)—we must not forget, then, that even if we take into account the differences in style and depth (or, conversely, in vulgarity and stupidity), the terrain and the stakes are the *same,* the project is the *same,* the strategy is the *same.* "The same," indeed, but not "identical." I am not pronouncing a massive—that is, a "moral"—condemnation: that is not my primary concern for the moment. I am simply making a statement. When, in 1935, Heidegger pronounces the word *mythology* without the slightest reservation, I cannot fail to hear the voice of Rector Krieck (for example), somewhere in the background, causing "interference" (a *Verstellung*, certainly . . .), as in the wireless radio of the time. In fact, with the 1953 edition of the same work, *Introduction to Metaphysics*, Heidegger will make it perfectly clear that he never thought of himself as anything other than "disappointed" by National Socialism. (In any case, I leave this formula to all its political triviality and inconsistency.)

The second reason is no less stupefying. The irruption of this word *mythology*—which, to my knowledge, is unique, a pure *hapax*, at least with this heavily laden valorization—occurs in relation to the problem of the "inception" (*Anfang*), the beginning or the origin of History: *Ur-Geschichte*, a term that Heidegger is careful to break down into its component parts so that we will not hear it merely as the end of prehistory or the birth of history (of "historical consciousness," of the writing and recording of facts, royal genealogies, etc.). The *"Ur"* of *Ur-Geschichte* is understood here in its transcendental sense. But of all the motifs relating back to *Being and Time* (chapter 5, section 72 ff.) and feeding directly into the political preaching of 1933, the motif of the beginning is unquestionably the dominant one. In the "Rectoral Address," this is the theme that, beyond its more narrowly academic concerns (which in effect repeat those of the Inaugural Lecture of 1929),[7] underlies the appeal to the "German people" to let itself be *led* "by the inexorability of that spiritual mission that forcefully stamps its proper historial character on its destiny."[8] Such a mission can be accomplished, says Heidegger, only on the condition that "we"—a "we" who is not simply the subject of the academic community—that *we Germans,* then, "place ourselves once again under the power of the *beginning* of our spiritual-historical Dasein," that is, under the power of the initial Greek irruption of *technē*, interpreted first of all as knowledge and science, *sophon,* and thus inevitably as "philosophy." Heidegger says, "This beginning is the irruption [*Aufbruch*][9] of Greek philosophy. It was there that for the first time Western man, on the basis of being-a-people [*Volkstum*] and by virtue of that people's language, rises up to face beings as a whole, that he questions them and grasps them as the beings that they are."[10] Now what does it mean to place oneself under the power of the Greek beginning? It means resolutely conforming to the "distant injunction to regain the greatness of the beginning." Heidegger continues, "For, assuming that the original Greek science is something great, then the *beginning* of this great thing remains its greatest moment. [. . .] The beginning still *is*. It does not lie *behind* us as something long past, but it stands *before* us. The beginning has—as the greatest moment, which exists in advance—already passed indifferently over and beyond all that is to come and hence over and beyond us as well. The beginning has invaded our future; it stands there as the distant injunction that orders us to recapture its greatness."[11]

We recognize here the very scheme of historicity articulated in *Being and Time* (in section 76, where Heidegger does not forgo an explicit reference to the second of Nietzsche's *Untimely Meditations*) in relation to the analysis of the three temporal ecstasies: Just as Dasein relates to the abyss of its present only insofar as, thrown toward its future, it is sent back to its past, that is, to the "invention" of its past; similarly, a possibility of History can be opened in the breach of the present only insofar as a people projects as (its) coming a possibility from its past that has not arrived or has remained concealed. In its greatness, or in what the *Introduction to Metaphysics* will call its *Unheimlichkeit*—which we could translate as its originary not-being-at-home—the Greek beginning harbors the possibility that will in no way be exhausted by the "development" that follows it or from which it proceeds, and that as such—that is, as still intact or unharmed—always awaits its manifestation and its effectuation. That is why the opening of History, the (re)beginning, is a repetition or retrieval (*Wiederholung*) of what did not yet arrive or begin in the beginning itself, of its failure to be truly initiating. Three years after the Rectoral Address, after the step has been taken—within the framework of the interpretation of *technē*—from an ontology of work (*energeia* understood as *am Werk sein*) to an ontology of art (*energeia* understood as *ins Werk setzen*), this very logic is in no way dismantled; it remains operative. As examples I will cite a few propositions from the final pages of "The Origin of the Work of Art" (but I could just as easily cite, once again, the *Introduction to Metaphysics* or the 1934–35 course on the *Hölderlin's Hymns*):[12]

> Bestowal and grounding [*Gründung*] have in themselves the abruptness of what we call a beginning [*Anfang*]. But this suddenness of the beginning, [. . .] includes [. . .] the fact that the beginning has inconspicuously prepared itself over the longest time. As a leap [*Sprung*], the genuine beginning is always a leaping-ahead [*Vorsprung*] in which everything to come is already leapt over [*übersprungen*],[13] even if as something veiled. Concealed within itself, the beginning already contains the end. A genuine beginning, of course, is not a beginning in the sense of being primitive. The primitive, because it lacks the bestowing, grounding leap and the leap-ahead, has no future. It cannot release anything more from itself, since it contains nothing save that in which it is caught.
>
> A beginning, by contrast, always contains the undisclosed fullness of the extraordinary [*des Ungeheures*], and that means the strife [*Streit*] with the ordinary [*mit dem Geheuren*].[14]

It is relatively unimportant here that this scheme of historicity (or historiality) and of (re)beginning (or initiality) survived its political "enlistment"—if it did not *in fact* authorize the latter. Indeed, it seems absolutely essential that such an "enlistment" took place not only in the wake of a tradition inaugurated by Nietzsche and transmitted by *Being and Time,* but was inscribed within a sort of "obsession" that Herder, first of all, and then a large part of Romantic historiography, had long established as the principle of "German ideology," understood here as the *doxa* of the Pan-Germanic far right, reinforced by the Napoleonic wars and the Treaty of Vienna (and then, of course, what followed . . .).

Here is another quote, from a few paragraphs later:

> Whenever art happens, whenever, that is, there is a beginning, a thrust [*Stoss*] enters history and history either begins or resumes. History, here, does not mean a sequence of events in time. [. . .] History is the transporting of a people into its appointed task as the entry into its endowment. [. . .]
>
> Art is history in the essential sense: It is the ground of history.
>
> Art allows truth [it is of course a question of *alētheia*—L.-L.] to

arise [*entspringen*]. Art arises [*erspringt*] as the founding preservation[15]
of the truth of beings in the work. To allow something to arise [*etwas
erspringen*], to bring something into being from out of the essential
source in the founding leap [*im stiftenden Sprung*] is what is meant by
the word "origin" [*Ursprung*].

The origin of the artwork—of, that is, creators and preservers [*der
Bewahrenden*], which is to say, the historical *Dasein* of a people—is art.
This is so because, in its essence, art is an origin.[16]

What is important, then, beyond the heavy political weight of these
statements, is not even the glacial and embarrassingly reflexive contempt for a supposed "primitivism." (On this point, the first version
of these lectures on "The Origin of the Work of Art" (1935) is even
more ridiculous in its indigent, self-satisfied "ethnocentrism," which
is not for a moment suspected as such, much less interrogated. Indeed,
this attitude, in its rather unexpected "progressivism" and its revolutionary "radicalism," does not exclude the political aspect.)[17] What is
really important here is that the task or the mission of beginning falls
henceforth to art and (almost) to art alone. For if, on the other hand,
the knowledge of originary History, of *Ur-Geschichte*, belongs entirely
to mythology, then it becomes quite clear that art, precisely as the power
of (re)beginning, is essentially myth.

Never—again, to my knowledge—does Heidegger say this *explicitly*. Which is to say that the word *muthos* is never used without being
placed in quotation marks: as a pure and simple quotation of the Greek
word, or as a reference to the frequent philosophical or "ideological"
use (a scholarly use in any case) that his contemporaries made of the
word—contemporaries whom I will call "Nietzschean," although of
course ideological Nietzscheanism has very little to do with what Nietzsche wrote *in truth*, and I am far from the first to argue this.

That said, we must be clear (which, after all, is not so frequent in
these matters): In these same pages on the origin of the work of art,
regardless of any differences between versions, once it has been posited
that art is essentially *Dichtung* (poetry), that is, *Sprache* (language),
then language in its essence is determined as "naming" (*nennen*) and
"saying" (*sagen*). But saying is here nothing other than "a projection
of the clearing in which it is said how being arrives in the open and

as what."[18] Language's saying is therefore, in turn, nothing other than *technē* itself, knowledge as origin, what I have on several occasions called "originary *technē*." But this knowledge or this *technē* now belong essentially to *Dichtung:* to "Poetry [...] thought here in such a broad sense, and at the same time in such an intimate and essential unity with language and the word, that it must remain open whether art [*Kunst*] in all its modes, from architecture to poesy [*Poesie*], exhausts the essence of poetry [*Dichtung*]."[19] And this Poetry itself, once again in its turn, is defined precisely as *die Sage: muthos* in Greek; or *fabula* in Latin: the "fable" in the sense in which Hölderlin—not just any example—used this word: "The fable, the poetic aspect of History and the architectonic of Heaven, is of great concern to me at the moment, especially the nationell, insofar as it is different from the Greek."[20] Translated into the Heideggerian idiom, this amounts to the following:

> Projective saying [*Sagen*] is poetry: the fable [*Sage*][21] of world and earth, the fable of the arena of their strife and, thereby, of every site of the nearness and distance of the gods. Poetry is the fable of the unconcealment of beings. The prevailing language is the happening of that saying in which its world rises up historically for a people and the earth is preserved as that which remains closed. Projective saying is that in which the preparation of the sayable at the same time brings the unsayable as such to the world. In such saying, the concepts of its essence—its belonging to world-history, in other words—are formed [*geprägt*], in advance, for a historial people.[22]

Such a fable or myth constitutes an origin for the historial *Dasein* of a people, thus giving it the *Prägung,* the imprint or the stamp, the "type" (*tupos*) of its mode of being in History. Its *type,* quite simply, along with the heavily political burden (to say no more than that) carried by this word—or by this ideologeme of the 1930s. In reference to the Platonic treatment of myth in book 2 of the *Republic*—which Heidegger would here be inverting or overturning without further ado—I decided some time ago to speak of a "typographic" function of myth, which seemed to me to be subtended by an "onto-typology."[23] Myth is effective and active, that is, exemplary, only because it imprints or impresses a *hexis,* in general, or a *habitus,* a style of existence, if you like, or an *ethos* (Nietzsche had refashioned the concept based on an overview of all the great Western "moralities" that emerged since the early Greeks). Such an onto-typology is visibly at work here as well. It marks Heidegger's thought and its lexicon (*Prägung, Schlage, Geschlecht,* particularly in the commentary on Trakl, etc.). It is perhaps the site of Heidegger's greatest resistance to his own project of "deconstruction," a resistance that we find at work in his stubbornest "political" impulses.

Myth would thus be the historial inscription of a people, and the means by which a people is able to identify itself or appropriate itself as such, to see its world—and in particular its state—established or instituted, to receive and respect the gods, or even to entrust itself to them or to let itself be ruled by them—having nonetheless previously imposed them: that is, figured or "fictioned" them. And this is the function that Heidegger assigns to the "linguistic work" (or the "work of speech": *Sprachwerk*) when, in the lectures of 1935–36, he repeats Hegel from the article on "Natural Law" or from the chapter on *Sittlichkeit* ("The Ethical Order") in the *Phenomenology of Spirit,* "The same is true of the linguistic work. In tragedy, nothing is staged or displayed theatrically. Rather, the battle of the new gods against the old is being fought. When the linguistic work arises from the saying of the people, it does not talk about this battle. Rather, it transforms that saying so that now every essential word fights the battle and puts up for decision what is holy and what unholy, what is great and what small, what is brave and what cowardly, what is noble and what fugitive, what is master and what slave (cf. Heraclitus, Fragment 53 in Diels, *Fragmente der Vorsokratiker*)."[24] That, then, is how the guiding concepts of the existence of a people brought back to its proper essence are "formed" or "imprinted in advance." And it is not only the analogy between the German *sagen/Sage* and the Greek *muthein/muthos* (or even the Latin *fari/fabula*) that authorizes us to think that it is indeed a question of myth. It is not only that the *Sage* concerns the conflict or combat between earth and world, or between what the philosophical tradition has called *phusis* and *technē,* nature and art, nature and culture (or history), etc. It is that the *Sage* is at the same time, if not beforehand, a *Sage* "of all proximity or of all distancing of the gods." The Poem, for Heidegger, is a Mytheme, and will remain so up to the end, because it is essentially *theological,* even when it has nothing to say but the absenting of the divine or the de-divinization of the world (its *Entgötterung,* so deliberately similar, in the 1930s, to Max Weber's *Entzauberung* [disenchantment]). "Even the doom of the absence of the god is a way in which world worlds," says Heidegger in one of the lectures of 1936.[25] And we know indeed that, even without (re)considering the famous "testamentary" judgment from 1966 ("Only a god can save us now," etc.) or, symmetrically and inversely, the stubborn denial of all religiosity (the *religio* is a Roman concept, etc.), myth, for Heidegger, is nothing other than the opening or the possibility of the sacred (or the holy) and, as such, it is an *index*—strictly understood in terms of the Greek *deixis,* the Latin *dictamen,* the German *Dichten,* or on the basis of an antilinguistic valorization of *Zeigen* over *Zeichen,* of "showing" over "signifying"—myth is the index, then, both of an intensified vindication of *Logic* and a pathos-laden haunting by *Religion.* At the same time, I would ask, provisionally, that we not be too quick to see these two terms as coinciding purely and simply with what Heidegger himself delimited under the name of *onto-theology* in order to designate the unfolding of Western metaphysics in its entirety.

This "prologue" is not the place to insist on this. That is why I will limit myself to recalling, for the record, a few propositions from Heidegger's later courses (after he was reintegrated into the university system in 1951). These propositions will require more detailed analyses on another occasion:

> Saying, for the Greeks, means to make manifest, to make appearing appear along with what is in appearing, what is in its epiphany.
>
> *Muthos* is that which, in its saying, is: it is that which appears in the unveiling of its appeal.
>
> *Muthos* is the appeal that touches the entire being of man radically and in advance, the appeal that makes us think of the being that appears, that is. *Logos* says the same thing.[26]

> It is a prejudice of the history of philology, inherited from modern rationalism and on the basis of Platonism, to believe that *Muthos* was destroyed by *Logos.* [. . .] The religious is never destroyed by logic, but always only by the fact that the god withdraws.

It is true that Heidegger will make it a point explicitly to exclude every banal or vulgarly anthropologico-theological interpretation of *Sage*. Much later, in "The Way to Language," the last lecture[27] included in *On the Way to Language,* he will insist on a clarification: "We have a tendency today to use the word *Sage,* like so many other words in our language, mostly in a disparaging sense. *Sage* is considered a mere saying-so, an unsupported and hence untrustworthy rumor. Here *die Sage* is not understood in this sense, nor is it taken in the sense of *die Götter- und Heldensage,* the 'saga of gods and heroes.' [. . .] In keeping with the most ancient usage of the word we understand *die Sage* in terms of showing."[28] This is followed, in fact, by a restatement, in a somewhat different formulation, of the earlier analysis of the *logos apophantikos* from *Being and Time* and of what the lectures on the work of art established as the essence of *Dichtung.*

But this warning that we should not confuse *Sage* with "saga," in the Scandinavian and German (and, at bottom, Wagnerian) sense of the term, hardly prevents us from seeing it as a reworking of the very concept of *muthos,* a reworking no doubt intended, in fact, to render it incompatible with the openly fascist vindication of *muthos* against *logos,* itself identified with *ratio.* In any case, it did not prevent Heidegger, beginning in the first courses on Hölderlin in 1934, from referring the "mysterious" origin of language—or of a particular language—to Homer, or from assigning to him the origin of a mystery (*Geheimnis*) as impenetrable—that is, as undisclosable—as the mystery of the *unheimlich* beginning, which is precisely what leads to the disclosure of that which alone *can* be disclosed from the undisclosable. (As Heidegger liked to point out, the word for art, *die Kunst,* comes from *können,* to be able.)

For the sake of economy, I will remain with the *Introduction to Metaphysics:*

> In the question of the essence of language, the question of the origin of language surfaces again and again. One looks for an answer in the most peculiar ways. And here we have the first, decisive answer to the question of the origin of language: This origin remains a mystery—not because people up to now were not clever enough but because all cleverness and

all sharp wit have mishandled the question before they even get started with it. The character of a mystery belongs to the essence of the origin of language. But this implies that language can have begun only from the overpowering and the uncanny [*aus dem Überwältigenden und Unheimlichen*], in the irruption of humanity into being. In this irruption, language was the becoming-word of being: poetry [*Dichtung*]. Language is the primal poetry [*Urdichtung*] in which a people poetizes or dictates [*dichtet*] Being. In turn, the great poetry by which a people steps into history begins the figuration [*Gestaltung*] of its language. The Greeks created and experienced this poetry through Homer. Language was revealed [*offenbar*] to their *Dasein* as an irruption into being, as a revelatory figuration of beings [*als eröffnende Gestaltung des Seienden*].[29]

In its own style and vocabulary, this passage not only repeats Herodotus, whom Herder, Hegel, and Schelling (among others) had already repeated, each in his own way; with obvious complacency, it also plays on a "religious" overdetermination derived, at least, from a certain Christianity: *Mysterium magnum* and *Offenbarung,* Revelation. Nothing, then, assures us that *Sage* is anything other than myth in the most prevalent sense of "mythology"—particularly if we keep in mind both the convoluted strategy pursued by Heidegger in relation to Nazism and the *apophansis* of fundamental ontology. The Poem is originary, both as language and as poetry, to the extent that it is, in a direct and immediate way, the myth by which a people is "typed" in its historial existence. The origin is properly mythical or, if you prefer, the beginning requires the forceful emergence of a "founding myth." And, in sum, if we reduce these propositions to their most trivial dimension, we see that they contain perhaps nothing other than what all modern Europe has dreamt of since the Reformation, most often in an academic form (illustrated in the most painful way by the nineteenth century), under the name of a "national epic." How paltry, and how poor.

It is at this point, however, that I would like to pose a *question*; for it is by no means a judgment that I want to pronounce. This question, moreover, is perhaps a little too simple—a little too "elementary." But it still seems to me absolutely indispensable to ask it. It is not unrelated to a *necessity* of our age.

Seen, if I may say so, from "our" perspective, interrogated after the fact and henceforth with an ample knowledge of what was at stake, Heidegger's gesture with respect to myth might seem to result not from his political errors and compromises—in fact the opposite is the case—but from an overdetermination that for now, and despite myself, I cannot describe as anything other than "ideological." It is a gesture that one could designate very roughly as "national-modernist," or, if we think of Hölderlin's peculiar way of understanding the French spoken in 1789, "nationell-modernist," where the Modern should be understood, in conformity with the Hölderlinian interpretation, as the repetition of what did not happen in the Ancient—and art, or politics, or both together, should be understood as the anamnesis of the forgotten or the remembrance of what is originarily "potential" but absent. And yet, for all that, we must no doubt avoid a misunderstanding: This gesture that, *today,* seems to us so dubious and slippery can also be seen as a clear and forceful reminder: any mythological *reconstitution* is illusory, erroneous, and indigent. The myth that National Socialism wanted to claim, and that an entire "German ideology" had wanted to claim before it or behind it, is in no way myth in its essence, but rather myth insofar as it can be represented, from the very point of view of the dominant and contested rationality (in any case in the register of lost "values" and "meaning" that was predominant at the time)—that is, from the point of view of a feeble irrationalism resulting from a simple reversal of Platonism (but lacking Nietzschean probity). This kind of myth is never anything more than the symptom of a confused and wounded "protest." That is why, despite all appearances (and these are considerable), *Sage* is not the simple Germanization of *muthos,* which, however, cannot be said of its complacent transcription as *Mythos* by the "thinkers" of the Party, in their mechanical opposition to "calculating Reason" and to *Logos* (it would be necessary after all to read Rector Krieck, or even Walter Friedrich Otto). Certainly, Heidegger rethinks—and "repeats" in his manner—the German tradition of "remythologization." He is not entirely immersed in it.

Except, strangely, on one point: a certain "religiosity." I use this word only with the utmost prudence: beginning at least with the *Contributions to Philosophy,* in which the problem of a "new god" or a "coming god," not to say the "last god," is explicitly thematized, Heidegger, who did not abandon Catholicism for nothing (whatever form this abandonment may have taken: a simple distancing, a denial, a discovery of Bultmann and Reformation theology), could not find harsh enough words to say about "religion," a concept and a reality that he considered exclusively "Roman." But this rejection in no way excludes what (at least provisionally and for the sake of convenience) we can call "piety"; quite the opposite. It was not without a certain ostentation that a "sobered-up" postwar Heidegger manifested a sort of "pietism" marked by deep compunction and benevolent solemnity; he did this particularly in his "private" lectures or in a publication like the "Letter on 'Humanism,'" and by means of a surprising shift from a heroic and vindicating rhetoric to a tranquil and deliberately bland sermonizing. Such a maneuver is perfectly transparent: There is no more reliable method of "whitewashing" than this edifying posture. Devotion is hardly a recent weapon; in difficult periods, it is perhaps the only recourse: "What a saint!" And this would be the real *question*, which I will gladly call, and not only for that reason, "archi-political."

But when it comes to "pietism" in these conditions, or to the "mystical" withdrawal (or that of the rustic or the woodsman), what else could this be but what our contemporaries would call, in their own complacent and "facile" patois, a *soft* fascism? Or what for my part I would call a watered-down "archi-fascism," made to seem respectable, or in any case acceptable and compatible with any number of other politico-philosophical preferences.

It is decidedly necessary—and this is what in the end has oriented me here—to take up once again, on a new basis and in different terms, the question of the Poem's vocation, and not to abandon it to a disabused weariness or an obsessional resentment.

CHAPTER 1

❦ ❦ ❦   Poetry, Philosophy, Politics

Should poetry cease to be of interest to philosophy? Must we [*faut-il*]—as a necessity or an imperative—sever the tie that for two centuries in Europe has united philosophy (or at least that philosophy that is astonished at its origin and anxious over its own possibility), and poetry (or at least that poetry that acknowledges a vocation toward thought and is also inhabited by an anxiety over its destination)? Must philosophy—by necessity or imperative—cease its longing for poetry, and conversely (for there is indeed reciprocity here), must poetry finally mourn every hope of proffering the true, and must it renounce?

We would not be asking such a question, or we would be asking it differently, if Alain Badiou had not recently situated it at the very center of what is at stake today in philosophizing—in the very possibility of philosophizing.

In *L'Être et l'événement* (*Being and Event*), but in an even more precise and trenchant way in his *Manifesto for Philosophy*[1]—a title that after all speaks for itself—Badiou points to the end of what he calls "the age of the poets," an age, from Hölderlin to Celan, in which the Poem offers itself or lends itself exclusively, as it were, to philosophical discourse. Likewise, he argues that the proper task of philosophy, in asserting itself again as such, is to turn away from the Poem in order to devote itself to the Matheme, according to its original vocation; or, more precisely, its task is to reconstitute the entire initial fourfold structure of its conditions (consisting of politics, love, poetry, and mathematics). Reduced to these few words, this thesis seems much simpler than it really is; indeed, it is quite impressive in its comprehensiveness, in its assurance, and in the abruptness with which it attempts to overturn a tradition that Alain Badiou cannot be accused of ignoring or misunderstanding—and within which, by the way, he places me, along with a few others. Nonetheless, I consider this thesis "debatable." This means first of all that I have thought it necessary—and imperative—to submit it, and its author, to debate and discussion, and this on a number of occasions. (And I should say that these discussions have always been marked by the high regard in which I hold this thinker's thought.) But it also means that, despite these discussions, or because of them, I do not believe that this thesis is right, at least not in the terms in which it is stated. It is not right, both in the sense of correctness and in the sense of justice. That is why I would like to explicate and confront these questions here before you: This seems necessary to me today, or rather imperative. As Badiou himself knows very well, the stakes are immense: They involve nothing less than the very possibility, and perhaps the mutual exclusion, of poetry, philosophy, and politics. At least that is the legacy that has been transmitted to us by Heidegger—a legacy that is extraordinarily difficult to take up and to take on. But in this sense I very much agree with Badiou: There is no way to avoid taking a position.

For the sake of clarity, and in order to define the issues at stake, I would first like to recall briefly, but as faithfully as possible, Badiou's thesis and his project.

Central to Badiou's project, in fact, is an attempt to make philosophy possible once again, by taking a step beyond the declaration of its end or the designation (and delineation) of its closure. This attempt is presented, in a completely explicit way, as a repetition of Plato's (founding) gesture: Plato must—by necessity or imperative—be rebegun. Consequently, with regard to poetry, the no less foundational gesture of repudiation and exclusion must be repeated. As Jacques Rancière has said: "*Being and Event* explicitly calls for a reprise of the Platonic gesture: to dismiss the poets so that philosophy can provide the basis for a politics of truth."[2] I recall this formula because of the concise way in which it associates poetry, philosophy, and politics (though perhaps more in the manner of Plato than in that of Badiou himself).

In Badiou's terms, then, it has become necessary to "unsuture" philosophy from its (exclusively) poetic condition, which is only *one* of the four conditions that make up the entire field of the "generic procedures" in which philosophy originates. As a consequence, it is also a question of putting an end to (or of recognizing the end of) this age—the nineteenth century, if you like, and if we can extend the latter all the way to 1945, or even further—when philosophy, in order to unsuture itself from its exclusively scientific condition (positivism) or its exclusively political condition (Marx, the totalitarianisms), "handed itself over" to the Poem. Badiou says: from Nietzsche to Heidegger. (But I will return to this periodization in a moment. For now I will note simply that Badiou takes Heidegger seriously enough to claim that it is here, in this unsuturing, that we encounter the "central question" and the "supreme difficulty" still facing us today.)

Against this background, and in a mode that is after all very Heideggerian, Badiou defines the age of the poets also as that age, from Hölderlin to Celan, in which—over and against the culpable failure of philosophy—poetry became a work of thought and came to occupy that "site of language in which a proposition on being and time is put forth." It is an age in which poetry thus overturned (as Nietzsche put it) the Platonic determination of this "ancient rivalry." Poetry, then, as a supplement to philosophy. But now this age is past. As Badiou writes in the *Manifesto*: "Paul Celan's work states, at the terminal edge, and from within poetry, the end of the age of the poets. Celan completes Hölderlin."[3] That is why, in the order of events that today make it necessary to unsuture philosophy from (only) one of its conditions—and here we must take "event" in the sense intended by Badiou: as the taking-place of that-which-is-not-being-as-being, of the order of the supplement or of the supernumerary (since mathematics is the science of being-as-being), therefore as withdrawn from knowledge, undecidable or indiscernible, rebelling against every presentation and yet capable of being thought as a truth, actually and after the fact, and thus requiring intervention and fidelity—in the order of events, then, that oblige the unilateral unsuturing of philosophy, the work of Paul Celan is the event that calls upon us to think the necessary unsuturing of philosophy from the Poem. It is in this sense that Badiou interprets the encounter between Celan and Heidegger, "a quasi-mythical episode of our epoch,"[4] in which the poet is sent back—by the philosopher of the Poem—to the solitude of poetry.

That is the thesis, in its most general form. My intention is in no way simply to incriminate it. For one thing, it is based on such a far-reaching discussion (concerning ontology and the essence of philosophy, the Greek invention of the Matheme, Platonism and the meaning of modern anti-Platonism, the history of being, the transformation of modern mathematics, etc.) that to do so would require a very lengthy demonstration, which I could not present here in any case. I would simply like to articulate two or three questions, which will serve as an introduction to the argument that I would like to present.

First, just as one might suspect that Badiou relies on an overly restricted concept of philosophy (the Platonic definition or—and this amounts to the same thing—one that assigns ontology, the properly Western mode of thought, to mathematics), and that he thereby refuses an essential aspect of the Heideggerian determination of philosophy (of metaphysics), such that he contests the declaration of its "end"—likewise, I think, we should not be surprised that Badiou bases his claims on a relatively narrow delimitation of poetry. I am thinking in particular of the list in which he enumerates the poets of the "age of the poets" (concerning which Badiou is very careful to insist that it is not meant as any dispensation of honors), that is: Hölderlin, and then all those who, as Badiou points out, came after the Commune: Mallarmé, Rimbaud, Trakl, Pessoa, Mandelstam, and Celan. Although it locates its inaugural reference in Hölderlin, this list is obviously not the same as Heidegger's: missing are George and Rilke, or even Goethe and Mörike. But also the Greeks, especially Sophocles, which alone would be reason enough for Heidegger not to have recognized such a definition of the "age of the poets." He would have given it a completely different scope and would have plotted it out in a completely different way. But I also see that Celan, for his part, would have added Büchner ("The Meridian" is very clear in this respect); and Hölderlin, probably, would have included Rousseau—at least the Rousseau of the *Reveries,* which we can indeed consider as the initiating *envoi* of modern lyricism. There wouldn't be anything worth arguing about in all this, if an indication were not thus given of the entire stakes involved in the Idea of poetry as prose, as Benjamin articulated it in his reading of Hölderlin and Jena

Romanticism. And, as I will suggest, there are enormous philosophi-cal—which is to say political—stakes in this.

This first question—and it is a real question, not an objection—is closely connected to a second one. Alain Badiou writes in the *Manifesto:*

> Every suture is an exaggeration, for as I have repeated with Heidegger, philosophy aggravates the problems. Sutured to one of its conditions, philosophy ascribes to this condition virtues that would remain imper-ceptible from within the exercise of the condition itself. By isolating the poem as the sole figure of thought and risk and as the instantiation of distress and salvation that points toward a destiny; by going so far as to envision (after René Char) a "power of poets and thinkers," Heidegger exceeded the poetic jurisdiction, which does not legislate any such com-mon power to poets and thinkers—except when it "strikes a pose" (which is, alas, a little too often the case with Char). The poetic jurisdiction treats the matheme in particular—not to mention politics or love—in a completely different way. With respect to the poem, Heidegger has done nothing other than those—and I was one of them—who philosophically absolutized politics from within the Marxist suture, well beyond what the reality of politics was able to say about itself.[5]

The question that I would like to ask here is whether this philosophi-cal absolutizing of poetry—regardless of the "pose" (in the manner of René Char, but also of Rilke, George, and so many others . . .)—is not grounded somewhere other than in poetry alone. I am not thereby suggesting anything in particular about the distress proper to phi-losophy, at least in relation to science (but not, as Badiou suggests, in relation to politics). It seems to me rather that if such an absolutiz-ing occurred—and it undeniably did—it was based on philosophy's relation not to poetry itself, if such a thing can be isolated, but to the supposed provenance of poetry or to its native element—its origin and its essence, which is to say, myth (this, at any rate, is the hypothesis guiding me here), with all the religious, sacred, and sacralizing—but also very broadly "political"—connotations that this word implies.

I have one last question. Because he credits Heidegger's thought with having been up to now "the only one to grasp what was at stake in the poem, namely the destitution of object fetishism [which for

Badiou implies the legitimate "deconstruction of the theme of the subject"—L.-L.], the opposition of truth and knowledge, and finally the essential disorientation of our age,"[6] Badiou makes two remarks concerning the bond formed between poetry and politics as a result of the suturing of the Poem:

1. Heidegger's "stroke of genius"—to use Badiou's expression—was, among other things, "to have [. . .] reached the point where it is possible *to hand philosophy over to poetry.* This suture seems to be a guarantee of strength, for it is true that there was an age of the poets. The existence of the poets, without which Heidegger's thought would have been aporetic and hopeless, provided this thought with a ground of historicity and actuality capable of conferring on it—once the mirage of a political historicity had been concretized and dissolved in the Nazi horror—what was to be its only real occurrence."[7]

2. With regard to the encounter between Celan and Heidegger, Badiou remarks that Heidegger's question "what are poets for?" can become, for the poet, "what are philosophers for?" and that if the answer to this question is "so that there can be poets," then this only increases the poet's solitude—and one of the reasons that Celan's work is a major event is precisely because it asks, poetically, to be relieved of this solitude. And Badiou adds: "How could Heidegger shatter the mirror of the poem—which Celan's poetry does in its own way—, given that he did not believe himself capable of elucidating, in the order of political conditions, his own National Socialist engagement? This silence, aside from the fact that it gravely offended the Jewish poet, was also an irremediable philosophical omission, because it brought the reductive and annihilating effects of the suture to their height, and to an intolerable point. It was here that Celan might have come to experience the ultimate result to which the philosophical fetishism of the poem could lead."[8]

In these two remarks—in which, by the way, it seems to me that Badiou gives too much credit to Heidegger, who did not believe himself *incapable* of elucidating his own political engagement, in the order of political conditions, but rather, quite simply, he did not deem it his *duty* or as something to which he could justly *be held*—in these two remarks, then, Badiou does more than merely incriminate the philosophical suturing of the Poem. What he incriminates, if I can put it this way, is the suturing to the political of philosophy's suturing to the Poem. In any case, this is indeed what I am tempted to think; or at the very least it is in this direction that I would like to take my question. For it is clear that Badiou does incriminate the political effect—or sense—of the poetic suturing.

That, then, is the question I would like to put into play here, concerning this link between poetry, philosophy, and politics. Not in order to cast doubt on the concept of the suture or of suturing (I believe it is operative); but because it seems to me that the suturing of philosophy to the Poem, as Badiou analyzes it, as well as the corresponding desuturing (the Platonic one, for example), does not exactly concern poetry, and especially not poetry in its properly modern exigency. There is a sort of misunderstanding at work here, if you like, one that certainly does bear on poetry, but also on politics—or at least on a determinate type of politics, not to say a style, associated with the philosophy from which Badiou demarcates himself.

I have already alluded to this misunderstanding, which can be designated with one word: myth. It may be that, in reality, this suturing did not happen to, or was not imposed upon, the Poem, but rather the Mytheme. And it is on this basis that a certain very determinate politics, indeed, may have been engaged. That, at least, is what I would like to demonstrate. But we see immediately how extensive the analysis required by such a demonstration would have to be. That is why I will limit myself to a few propositions that I hope are not too dry or rigid, but which will inevitably remain somewhat elliptical. Or pragmatic.

My first proposition is that the destiny that bound poetry, philosophy, and politics together, each to each and to both of the others—and in an essential mode—took shape on two occasions in our history or in our tradition, and that, in each case, it was a question of the very possibility of philosophy. The first time was nothing less than the inauguration of philosophy strictly speaking; the second time occurred at the beginning of a no doubt irreversible process leading to the final completion—in every sense—of philosophy.

If I thus restrict this entire long history and its immense complexity to these two moments—in which these relations, in my opinion, emerged in an essential mode—it is because I believe it possible to indicate that in both cases, at a time when poetry itself existed within a previously established relation to political reality, it suddenly appeared to philosophy as a *question* (which in itself is highly significant), and that this question, which may be an altogether primal one, is quite simply for philosophy the question of its own chances for life or survival—to the extent, moreover, that this life (or this survival) is in turn bound up with securing a hegemonic position at the heart of the political.

What allows us to formulate this thesis—which is rather sweeping, I admit—is of course the text of Plato; but it is also the repetition (a certain repetition), in the Hegelian discourse, of the "scene" that Plato handed down to posterity. It is a repetition in which the destiny I am speaking of took shape for a second time, although in a completely different way.

With regard to Plato, I will limit myself to a few reminders. Despite everything, I believe they are necessary; and they will allow me to articulate a second proposition.

Everyone recalls at least this much: There is a legend, repeated as late as Nietzsche, saying that Plato—as Mallarmé said of Rimbaud—surgically removed [*opéré*] poetry from his living body: at the instigation of Socrates, it is said, Plato burned his tragic poems. And there is a scene that is in many respects the "primal scene" of philosophy: the ritual expulsion, in book 3 of the *Republic,* of the tragic poet-actor, treated in the end and in a very "spectacular" fashion as a *pharmakos.* A self-mutilating operation, a purifying fire, or a sacrificial gesture—in any case, philosophy thus organizes itself and sets itself into a work [*se met en oeuvre*] (if we can give any credence to the semantic background of the word "operation"); it is born from the ashes of poetry, or it sanctions, in a politico-religious ceremony, the rejection of the very thing that seems to have threatened philosophy in its most essential project. This project is the political project itself (and this is also revealed in the last book of the *Laws*: the most beautiful tragic poem, we read, is precisely here, in this constitution, and we are the ones who composed it):[9] namely, the project of the philosophical *basileia,* which, as Heidegger recalled in 1936, does not mean that the philosophy professors should be set up as commanders of the state, but that philosophy's vocation is to ensure that the state is instituted *in truth.*

These are questions with which we are familiar; they are inscribed within our philosophical—and not only our philosophical—memory. We know that philosophy (strictly speaking) is *decided,* in the strongest sense, in this break with poetry, which is in fact first of all—and this is never sufficiently emphasized—a break with the theater (dramatic poetry) and with *mimēsis* as a daimonic and primal mode of enunciation. (I note in passing that with respect to lyricism, particularly Pindar, Plato does not show nearly the same severity. Certainly, Plato dislikes art. He rejects it. But this does not necessarily mean that he detests poetry, in the sense that we understand this, practically speaking: the poetry that is not "literature.") And we are of course familiar with all the stakes involved: They are indissociably pedagogical, religious, and political. They concern the ancient (archaic) aristocratic *paideia* (education through heroic examples), a religion judged to be false and obsolete, and a state with no true founding principle or project. The task assumed by what is thus born under the name of philosophy is consequently that of redressing these errors: It is an *orthopedic* task that, henceforth, philosophy will almost always consider a necessity. We find here an entire program, in fact, but unlike other programs derived from other gestures of philosophical decision (in relation to the Sophists for example), this program succeeded, at least in the sense that art (including poetry, but perhaps not all the arts) remained definitively subordinate—given that a pure and simple exclusion was strictly utopian. In the West, art (but not necessarily the Poem) will always be under surveillance: at first by a *poetics,* certainly (but why exactly is it that what remains from Aristotle's teaching on these questions is only the examination of tragedy?); but especially by what will end up being called *aesthetics.* For I think that Heidegger was correct to say that, in principle, aesthetics is first founded in the Platonico-Aristotelian apprehension of art.

But when Plato carries out this operation, he authorizes his arguments with reference to a more ancient differend: a *palaia diaphora,* he says, and I do not think that this is meant merely to shift the guilt away from himself. After all, it is true that Heraclitus, for example, shows little affection for Homer. Where did this differend lead? Not all the hypotheses on this question are equally convincing.

The hatred of the theater is almost certainly something specific to Plato, and the theater is indeed directly political, if we think for a moment about what the institution of tragedy represented in Athens. Nietzsche was right in this respect. But if Plato's specific contribution thus turns out to be the analysis of *lexis* (the modalities of enunciation), then the discrimination between two regimes of *legein* (the true and the false), or rather between two registers of speech (*muthos* and *logos*), does indeed seem to be the legacy on which he draws in order to ground his uncompromising critique of what he calls *muthopoiesis* and to ensure the hegemonic position of what he vindicates under the name of philosophy. In reality, what Plato excludes, more than the theater and all the forms of mimetic or semimimetic enunciation, is myth.

Such a critique is political nonetheless—indeed, if only because it so directly takes on the Greeks' *religion* (a term on which I insist). And with such violence. But precisely in that sense—and this is my second proposition here—this critique definitively associates poetry in its highest destination with religion, and it does so in terms of *muthopoiesis*. That is at least how Plato has virtually always been read. This is why, at the end—or close to the end—of the tradition that followed, Hegel can speak of the "religion of art" in reference to the Greek moment; likewise, it is what provides the Romantics (Schlegel, Novalis) with a basis for their desire to institute a "new religion" founded on poetry (on *Dichtung*). After two thousand years of the versification against which Rimbaud vituperated, poetry attempts to respond once again to this vocation that is more than political—I would say: *archi-political*. But perhaps it does so to its own detriment and misfortune, if this vocation is definitively dictated to it by philosophy. I am thinking of Hölderlin, or again of Rimbaud.

In the meantime, however, another event was necessary within philosophy itself. Hence my third proposition.

The event I am referring to here is the Kantian critique, or its systematic "repetition" in Fichte's *Science of Knowledge*.[10] The Schlegels, who did not speak lightly on such matters, placed this critique alongside the French Revolution (in the order of the political) and Goethe's *Wilhelm Meister* (in the order of the poetic), as that event which, in the order of the philosophical, marked a new age, a change of epoch. If we can ascribe such a fate to the Kantian critique, it is less because it is a critique (and the first time that metaphysics calls itself into question) than because in order to be such, that is, to be critical, the critique must recall metaphysics as a whole *ab initio*. In this respect, the critique is the first philosophical anamnesis of philosophy, and therefore the first repercussion after the fact—in the figure of lucidity—of the Platonic decision.

Here, then, for the second time, we see the destiny in which philosophy, poetry, and politics were bound together—each to each and to both of the others. And this happened almost immediately (or in any case immediately after the publication of the third *Critique*) and in a way that was completely prodigious. For it was in Romanticism—let us use this term as shorthand for everything that happened in Jena in the last decade of the eighteenth century—that the properly modern destination of *Dichtung* was invented (along with our concept of literature, which henceforth included poetry).

It would of course be necessary to introduce infinite nuances and to undertake analyses that would be equal to the complexity of these matters. But perhaps it is possible simply to provide an overview, however schematic. And in order to provide this overview, I believe that the three possibilities presented within the space opened by the Kantian critique can be emblematized by the three names of the fellow students at the Tübingen *Stift*: Hegel, Schelling, and Hölderlin. They delimited the territory from which we come; perhaps they still delimit the territory we are surveying today—or in which we move, apparently without borders or directions.

I hope that you will not object if I give less importance here to what appeared, under the name of Hegel, as a reaction pure and simple (I am thinking of the vulgate, including Marx, that was so powerful) and consequently as the renewal or the reaffirmation of the Platonic decision: art is "a thing of the past"; poetry is the moment of art's "dissolution"; in the "sad realm of the concept," our interest in and our need for the absolute cannot be satisfied by art or even by revealed religion; all the "seriousness of existence" has passed into matters of public life (into politics, if not into administration) and into the fulfillment of the Knowledge that grounds them in reason.

This version would have to be amended: Hegel's certainty is never simply certainty; and his lamentation over the end of art—the disappearance of life, or of a certain life—is genuine. Heidegger is certainly justified in suspecting that the Hegelian grasp of art depends on the Platonic apprehension of the being as *eidos.* Hegel completes Plato, deliberately, and sanctions the reign of the Idea. Nevertheless, the Hegelian *habitus* is not at all the same as that of Plato: Hegel truly pities Schiller for having to "pay tribute to the age" and for being the victim of the philosophical (aesthetic) sublation of art. Schiller is not Sophocles, nor even Shakespeare. But if two (slightly altered) lines of his poetry are used to punctuate, *in fine,* the last section of the *Phenomenology of Spirit* ("Absolute Knowledge"), this is perhaps not entirely a matter of ornamentation. Such a conclusive recourse to the Poem is perhaps—who knows?—abyssal.

But it is Schelling and Hölderlin that I would like to dwell on for a moment here: the first because he very clearly summarizes the Romantic project (the very one, it seems to me, that Badiou misapprehends), even down to its systematic aspect; the second because he indicates another route, one which he himself was perhaps unable to follow, and which, indeed, perhaps no one after him was able to follow (although I am doubtful of this). It is a route determined by a completely different reworking of the relation between philosophy, poetry, and politics. This is something that becomes visible if one is willing to see it, but that Heidegger, for his part, gravely misapprehended.

The project formulated by Schelling was condensed into these few lines, which conclude the *System of Transcendental Idealism* of 1800:

> But now if it is art alone which can succeed in objectifying with universal validity what the philosopher is able to present in a merely subjective fashion, there is one more conclusion yet to be drawn. Philosophy was born and nourished by poetry in the infancy of knowledge, and with it all those sciences it has guided toward perfection; we may thus expect them, on completion, to flow back like so many individual streams into

the universal ocean of poetry from which they took their source. Nor is it in general difficult to say what the medium for this return of science to poetry will be; for in mythology such a medium existed, before the occurrence of a breach now seemingly beyond repair. But how a new mythology is itself to arise, which shall be the creation, not of some individual author, but of a new race [*Geschlecht*],[11] personifying, as it were, one single poet—that is the problem whose solution can be looked for only in the future destinies of the world, and in the course of history to come.[12]

These lines would require a long commentary, particularly concerning the necessity—in view of the system's completion, that is, its real (historical and political) actualization—of objectifying the subjective sphere and what post-Kantian Idealism called "intellectual intuition" or "originary intuition": meta-physical intuition itself. And for Schelling this involves the entire difficult problem of the relation between the conscious and the unconscious, or between freedom and necessity (which practically speaking amounts to the same thing). But what I would like to underscore, very simply, is that this program—whose very terms echo the enigmatic text (by whom? Schelling? Hegel? Hölderlin?) in which, for the first time, the "system-program of German Idealism" was traced out[13]—that this program, then, has a political aim that will one day prove to be disastrous. Speaking of philosophy's return to poetry through the requisite mediation of a mythology (a "new mythology" or a "mythology of reason," as the "Oldest System-Program" of 1796 says), Schelling's *System* evokes a collective creation with the discreet term "generation"; in 1796, within the framework of the same project, it was a question of a people, and an appeal was made to a new *religion*. Is it necessary to insist on the disastrous consequences, after a century of vulgarization (particularly in the university), that this appeal (to a people) and this desire (for a religion) will have?

In any case, in the various overturnings of Platonism (on which Nietzsche holds no monopoly), in the anamnesis (the *Andenken*) and nostalgia that called up a more archaic and original Greece, more profound and more essential than the neoclassical Antiquity that ruled over Europe since the Renaissance (at least until the French Revolution, or even the Empire), and in the idea that only the German people—primarily because of its language—bears the promise of regaining the forgotten grandeur of this beginning: in all this there is the seed of a disastrous politics. And this disaster is inscribed—quite obviously, I'm afraid—in the very project of a "new mythology": a "myth of the future," as Nietzsche said at the time of *Zarathustra,* or a "myth of the twentieth century," as Rosenberg will say.

Rosenberg is obviously no Nietzsche. We can—we must—always save the thought of a great thinker. (And I do say the thought, which I do not confuse with actions, nor with political choices or simply preferences, nor with the consequences provoked by bad readings, including those for which the thinkers' readings of their own thought are responsible.) Bataille was right, in the 1930s, to insist so vigorously on the opposition separating Nietzsche and Rosenberg, even if there is a great deal that could be said about the *Acéphale* project, both the group and the journal. In any case, there remains a responsibility of thought. And this is something that is only aggravated in being denied.

That is why it is necessary [*il faut*] to make an exception of Hölderlin—and here the imperative indicates an urgency. Not only because it was as a poet and according to poetry that he took up the question of the relation between thought, poetry, and history, which for him was clearly the very question of poetry's possibility (as it will be, in a way that is in the end very similar, for Rimbaud and Mallarmé). But also because in Hölderlin we find: an extremely rigorous meditation on the difference between (Greek) enthusiasm and (Western) sobriety; a tragic acceptance of the law of finitude following from the "categorical turning away" of (and from) the divine; and a firm exigency regarding the difficulty—not to say the impossibility—of a "nationell" appropriation or identification (which, it must be acknowledged, was in fact underscored by Heidegger). All this ultimately forbids every form of *Schwärmerei* (out of fidelity to Kant), every poetic project founded exclusively in effusion, and every mythologization that would lead to the project of an immanent fashioning of a community. Despite everything.

Despite everything, I say, because on the other hand (and it would be pointless to conceal this) there are all the aspects that Heidegger exploited: the nostalgia for a Greece beset by the "fire of heaven" and subjected to the presence of the divine, the appearance of a "neopagan-ism," the sanctification of a poetic preaching, the belief in a possible reactivation of "legends" and the hope of singing "one day ... the forebears of our princes and their councils and the angels and the holy fatherland," that is, of giving to Germany its own song—or its myth.

But Hölderlin was too much of a Republican. He also had too great a sense of transcendence, even if this latter offered only the faceless face of its withdrawal. And especially, ruining all the preaching, there is the final disorganization of the work, the reworkings that reach the limits of the readable, the prosaic literalization of the discourse, as well as the fierce attack on the hymn and the desolation of the last poems. All of which Heidegger *refused* to read or—who knows?—did not even see ...

Hegel had little effect: Romanticism submerged European poetry, con-demning it for more than a century to all sorts of messianisms or prophe-tisms: republican and progressive, revolutionary and utopian, national-ist and antiquarian. The properly modern movements, the avant-gardes, submitted without exception to this overdetermination.

However, I think we can agree that the culmination of Romanti-cism—once again in an emblematic way, and with regard to its gravest political implications—is to be located in Wagner. And not only for Germany, as we know. This will be my final proposition.

The Romanticism that is in a certain way completed in Wagner—and that Nietzsche will eventually call resoundingly into question—does not, it is true, rest on its authentic metaphysical basis: A great distance separates Schelling from Schopenhauer. But from Romantic aesthetics Wagner retains at least the following:

1. The work of art "of the future," in its properly religious (which is to say political) function, and its vocation toward the self-representa-tion or the self-celebration of the people, must be founded on myth: for only myth is capable of giving a people the language and the figures in which to speak itself and recognize itself, that is, to identify (with) itself.

2. The great work, the "total artwork," has its model in tragedy and

in the Christian "sacred drama" (but let us not forget that the Mass, which also fascinated Mallarmé, was among the great models proposed by Schelling at the end of his *Philosophy of Art*).[14]

3. Every great art, as Greek art attests, is based on the opposition of two aesthetico-metaphysical principles or two powers, clearly identified since Schlegel, Hegel, and Hölderlin, but not definitively named until Nietzsche: the Dionysian and the Apollonian (here too, not without immediately producing the effect of a *vulgate* whose forms we are familiar with).

All this is perfectly consistent with what I would call the average project of Romanticism, whatever philosophical mutation may have occurred between speculative idealism and Wagner's use of Schopenhauer. But the clearest result of this completion is that, from the moment when the aim of the work is communal fusion (hysteria, Nietzsche will say), and when it seeks to evoke the vaguest metaphysical intuition—by as it were touching affect alone (emotion)—poetry becomes purely and simply subservient to music. Wagner's compositional techniques are well known in this respect. The metaphysico-political project of a new *myth* therefore leads, in a pure paradox, to the secondary status of *saying*, or (and this amounts to the same thing) to its false essentialization as *melos*—which would be infinite. Hence perhaps the exemplary character of the struggle waged by Mallarmé, who stubbornly defended the primacy of the Poem, that is, of language, and thus, on this point, redeemed Baudelaire's great weakness.[15] Hence, too, the exemplary character of all poetic attempts—however inevitable their demise—to renounce the excesses of the total or totalizing metaphysico-political project. I have mentioned Hölderlin, but I am also thinking of that testament to sobriety, Rimbaud's *Season in Hell,* and its "adieu" to the Romantic temptation (though in his case this took the far less objectionable form of a revolutionary utopia). At bottom this was a refusal of what Rimbaud, as if taking his vocabulary directly from both Hegel and Schelling, indissociably called Science and Magic.

Have we, then, dispensed with Romanticism? Despite its monstrous fulfillment (about which I hasten to say that I do not *simply* incriminate any of its great representatives) in what I am resigned to calling, for lack of a better term, "national-aestheticism,"[16] we are very aware of the weight exerted by an interpretation of poetry—in its relation to thought and its political ("historial") vocation—that is marked by a singular lack of lucidity with regard to the deepest thematics of Romanticism. And this is true even when it set out to interpret Hölderlin or Trakl—or even, toward the end, Rimbaud (though, to be sure, this was rather a misinterpretation).

With regard to Heidegger, since I am obviously referring to him, we no longer have the right either to simplify or merely to accuse. But it is necessary (and this is an imperative) to recognize the following:

1. After a certain disappointment (which was in fact real, there is no doubt about that), Heidegger's compromise was such as to lead him, in his vain or absurd attempt at a "rectification" of national socialism (in the sense, as you know, of its "internal truth" and "greatness," which had been thrown off course), to ground his thinking without any precautions in a very specifically oriented reading of Hölderlin. This reading is fundamentally *wrong,* even if Hölderlin, arrested at a certain stage—or at a certain stratum of his text—can lend himself to it.

2. Right up to his final texts, the interpretation of Hölderlin, but also of Trakl, moved in the direction of what I would call a "remythologization." We know the sequence: The essence of art is *Dichtung,* the essence of *Dichtung* is *Sprache* (both language and speech indissociably), the essence of *Sprache* is *Sage*—which is *muthos.* In the 1950s Heidegger may well say that *Sage* is not the *Heldensage,* the saga of heroes—and in fact, there is no Siegfried here; Heidegger's anti-Wagnerianism was always unshakable, which does distinguish him, after all. It is nonetheless the case that *Sage* translates nothing other than *muthos.* And there is something fundamentally *dubious* about this.

The essence of art, then, would be myth. This leaves us with one question, at least.

I believe that in this period of history to which we belong, we have reason to regret a certain "privatization" in poetry, a tendency toward the kind of idiomatic hermeticism that results from a renunciation if not of thinking, at least of a political or more broadly historical inscription. It is true that Europe is full of commotion, which is more and more evident every day. But can we, today, think a Poem without any Mytheme, one that has renounced neither thinking itself in its possibility (which no doubt amounts to thinking *tout court*), nor foretelling for human beings *what is necessary* [*ce qu'il faut*]—that is, *answering,* for their sake and in their favor, for what is necessary. Here too it is a question of an imperative.

We know that Celan, for one, never ceased his attempts to respond to such a question, and that these attempts involved a hand-to-hand struggle with Heidegger's overinterpretation of poetry.

Would Celan then be, for this reason, the end of the "age of the poets"?

The idea is not without some support. In the terms in which I have attempted to work through such a question, this would mean that "the age of the poets" came to a close with these two indeed desperate poems: "Tübingen, Jäner" and "Todtnauberg."[17] Somewhere between his renunciation of Hölderlin and his anger at Heidegger's (emphatically "poetic") silence. These would be two final poems that say the end of poetry as a "work of thought."

And yet, I am not so sure about this. To conclude, I would like to explain the origin of my suspicion.

In Germany in the 1930s, there were two ways of receiving Romanticism: The first, which was the most widespread at the time, was to welcome it in its entirety, although perhaps without really being aware of it, under the name of Nietzsche: it represented the great German tradition. The other, which was rarer and perhaps even limited to a single case, was to *treat* Romanticism and to take it seriously, philosophically speaking.

Heidegger more or less consistently represents the first way, all the more so—and all his philosophical seriousness is located here—in that he will do everything he can to combat Nietzsche, to situate speculative Idealism (to which he rigorously attaches Romanticism), and to demarcate Hölderlin from this historical, or historial, implication. And yet in doing this he renounces neither myth nor the religious vocation of the Poem. In 1935 Heidegger saw fit to assert that, in its origin, History falls under mythology, not paleontology. Twenty years later he will say that *muthos* gives way to *logos* only because the divine has withdrawn. And as late as 1946, he wrote the following, which in the end he never renounced:

> "German" is not spoken to the world so that the world might be re-formed through the German essence; rather it is spoken to the Germans so that from a destinal belongingness to other peoples they might become world-historical along with them [. . .]. The homeland of this historical dwelling is nearness to being.
>
> In such nearness, if at all, a decision may be made as to whether and how God and the gods withhold their presence and the night remains, whether and how the day of the sacred dawns, whether and how in the dawning of the sacred an apparition of God and the gods can begin anew. But the sacred, which alone is the essential sphere of divinity, which in turn alone affords a dimension for the gods and for God, comes to radiate only when being itself beforehand and after extensive preparation has been cleared and is experienced in its truth. Only thus does the overcoming of homelessness begin from being, a homelessness in which not only human beings but the essence of the human being wanders aimlessly about.[18]

These lines are from the "Letter on 'Humanism.'" They refer to Hölderlin, whose use of the word *das Deutsche* (the "German essence," as the translation puts it, or "Germanness") they exploit. A little earlier, Heidegger writes the following, which leaves no doubt about his interpretation:

> In the lecture on Hölderlin's elegy "Homecoming" (1943) this nearness "of" being, which the Da of Dasein is, is thought on the basis of *Being and Time*; it is perceived as spoken from the bard's poem; from the experience of the oblivion of being it is called the "homeland." The word is thought here in an essential sense, not patriotically or nationalistically, but in terms of the history of being. The essence of the homeland, however, is also mentioned with the intention of thinking the homelessness of contemporary human beings from the essence of being's history. Nietzsche was the last to experience this homelessness. From within metaphysics he was unable to find any other way out than an overturning of metaphysics. But that means definitively closing every possible way out. On the other hand, when Hölderlin composes "Homecoming" he is concerned that his "countrymen" find their essence. He does not at all seek that in an

egoism of his people. He sees it rather in the context of a belongingness to the destiny of the West.[19]

We know where this had recently led, despite everything. . . . The denials do nothing to change this.

The other way—the treatment of Romanticism, undertaken at some distance from Nietzsche—is that of Benjamin, who, however, was long fascinated by the George "circle" and was a commentator on Hölderlin beginning with the appearance of the large Hellingrath edition, but who was also the author, in 1920, of a dissertation on the concept of criticism in early Romanticism.

Presenting the argument in somewhat broad strokes, we could say that the paradox is the following:

What Benjamin wanted to articulate in Romanticism, as he admitted a number of times, was its esoteric heart or kernel, what he called its "messianism": the point, which he took to be central, where history and religion came to coincide, that is, where the secret desire to found a new religion—a desire that inhabited Romanticism—became manifest. Which is to say: a desire to found a new religion on the basis of art understood in its essence, that is, on the basis of *Dichtung*. This is familiar territory. But this is the same Benjamin who in the final pages of his dissertation addresses what Schlegel and Novalis called the "Idea of art" (thus providing an explication of the major concepts of the doctrine: poetry of poetry, universal progressive poetry, reflexive poetry, transcendental poetry, etc.) and who ends by showing that "the Idea of poetry is prose."

He is thinking, of course, of the fate that the Romantics assigned to the novel—particularly *Wilhelm Meister*. But he also knows that he is engaging in an interpretation, in the sense in which interpretation was for him a duty—an imperative—as he wrote to Scholem during the preparatory stages: "But Romanticism *must* be interpreted (with circumspection)."[20] Now, this interpretation comes down directly from Hölderlin, though not the Hölderlin to which we have become accustomed from Heidegger's interpretation—which is an interpretation as well, but not the same kind.

This is what Benjamin says:

This conception of the Idea of poetry as prose determines the whole Romantic philosophy of art. And it is this determination that has made the Romantic philosophy of art so historically rich in consequences. Not only did it spread with the spirit of modern criticism, without being "agnosticized" in its presuppositions or essence, but it also entered, in more or less clearly marked form, into the philosophical foundations of later schools of art. [. . .] Above all, however, this fundamental philosophical conception founds a peculiar relation within a wider Romantic circle, whose common element [. . .] remains undiscoverable so long as it is sought only in poetry and not in philosophy as well. From this point of view, one spirit moves into the wider circle, not to say into its center—a spirit who cannot be comprehended merely in his quality as a "poet" in the modern sense of the word (however high this must be reckoned), and whose relationship to the Romantic school, within the history of ideas, remains unclear if his particular philosophical identity with this school is not considered. This spirit is Hölderlin, and the thesis that establishes his philosophical relation to the Romantics is the principle of the sobriety of art. This principle is the essentially quite new and still incalculably influential leading idea of the Romantic philosophy of art; what is perhaps the greatest epoch in the West's philosophy of art is distinguished by this basic notion.[21]

To support this thesis, in which it is ultimately a question of the essence of modern literature, Benjamin cites at length the well-known opening section of Hölderlin's "Remarks on 'Oedipus,'" where the latter speaks of the "calculation" of the work. And he compares this intuition to many of the declarations made by Novalis and Schlegel: "Truly artistic poetry is numerable"; "art is mechanical"; "the seat of genuine art is solely in the intelligence"; "the true author [must be] a manufacturer," etc.[22] We are thus on the verge of the Matheme, as Badiou would say, who in fact does not fail to use similar declarations from Rimbaud, Lautréamont, or Mallarmé as a backdrop: "O, rigorous mathematics."[23] But the Matheme, if we follow Benjamin, is not the "mathematical." It is the Poem itself, that is, prose. Why should philosophy, or what remains of it, "unsuture" itself from the poem, if at the same time—and in the same movement—this can engage another politics, as the young Benjamin attests? And if prose—by which I mean poetry *as* prose—is, perhaps still today, "a new idea in Europe."[24]

CHAPTER 2

❦ ❦ ❦   *Il faut*

"To write, the exigency to write": The formulation is from Maurice Blanchot.[1] Such a formulation, and one can hear this immediately, touches on the very essentiality of what we can no longer have the nerve to name "literature" [la *littérature*]. And it does so without any commotion, almost modestly, but in a way that is altogether decisive. By means of this imperative without content, what was known as "literature"—a term that has authorized so many immense pretensions and inspired poses—is given over to its own naked existence as a fact and to a sort of duty without reason, much as the Rimbaud of *A Season in Hell* says that he is given over to the earth and to a harsh reality. In a register that is quite close to this (despite appearances), when Beckett was asked by a newspaper survey "Why do you write?" he gave this lapidary response: "Bon qu'à ça" ("It's all I'm good for").

In order to say this exigency, we have in our language—that is, in this French[2] that Hölderlin spoke a little and with which, in any case, he punctuated his late sketches and the last reworkings of his greatest poems—we have a formidable locution: *il faut* (it is necessary). Formidable but, undoubtedly, irreplaceable.[3]

The French word *falloir* ("to be necessary") derives—one can easily verify this—from the vulgar Latin *faillire,* itself based on the classical Latin *fallere:* to deceive, to elude, to be lacking. *Falloir* is thus a doublet of *faillir* ("to fail to . . ." in the sense of "almost to . . ."),[4] such that, in French, language makes it impossible for us not to hear in the very enunciation of an imperative or an obligation—in this injunction that is all the more binding for being, as one says, impersonal—, in this "il" *faut,* also *le défaut* (default, defect, lack), *la défaillance* (failure, weakness, breakdown), and *la faillite* (bankruptcy, collapse, failure). But also, and interminably, the imminence of a chance, the promise of a success or the admission of a failure (when there is only lacking [*il s'en faut*], precisely, an "almost," and this amounts also to a recognition of merit). And, it goes without saying, *la faute,* a fault in the sense of a mistake, an error, or an ethical lapse.

Since it is in this language alone, in French, that I am able to speak, I propose that we place Hölderlin—the oeuvre, if it is one, for which this name is a title—under the sign of the *il faut*: it is necessary.

We cannot forget, in fact, that in the one text among all the others in which he set down his highest and most difficult thought, in the "Remarks" on the translations of Sophocles, Hölderlin describes the tragic moment—that is, the moment in which "the becoming-one without limit" of the god and man "is purified by a separation without limit"—by indicating that the imperative itself, the categorical turning away of the god from man, must also be followed by man, that it is necessary for man to turn away as well: "man, because in this moment he must follow the categorical turning away" ("der Mensch, weil er in diesem Moment der kategorischen Umkehr folgen muss"). Man, too, is forced to turn away (it's the same word here as well: *umkehren*), "like a traitor, but indeed in a way that is holy."[5] It is as if the *il faut,* the "must" of the imperative, supposed and at the same time commanded a failure, a default or defection (Hölderlin speaks of infidelity), which are themselves the consequence of a fault, a transgression or a tragic excess. In his quite singular theology, Hölderlin would thus have brought to light the infinitely paradoxical logic, with no dialectical resolution, of the exigency that in French is concealed—but which exerts itself in a way that is indeed formidable—in the interval between *falloir* ("to be necessary") and *faillir* ("almost to . . ." or "to fail to . . ."), and which gives the *il faut* its strange resonance.

What I will attempt to articulate this evening, with you, is still at the stage of a sketch. In a work I am engaged in, I am pursuing a two-sided project. On the one hand I would like to respond to the decree, delivered in a Platonico-Hegelian mode, which Alain Badiou has pronounced concerning "the end of the age of the poets."[6] By "the age of the poets" Alain Badiou means an epoch, between Hölderlin and Celan, in which poetry—at least in a few bodies of work, very few really: seven, a sort of "pléiade"—assumed the task of providing a supplement to a failing philosophy that, during the same period, forgot the full scope of its "generic procedures" and "sutured" itself exclusively to only one of its conditions, whether science (that is, positivism) or politics (that is, in a word, what can be referred to as the philosophies of totalitarianism). It is therefore the age of a "thinking poetry," to use a Heideggerian phrase, and therefore the age in which, likewise, philosophy—at least that philosophy whose rigorous exigencies demanded that it refuse such sutures—oriented itself toward poetry in order to find in it the chance and the promise of thought. To which Heidegger, of course, attests in an exemplary fashion. And this is, moreover, the reason that Badiou sees in Celan's visit to Todtnauberg, and in his disappointment with the famous dialogue between the poet and the thinker, the emblematic figure of an end.[7]

But, on the other hand, because I am more and more persuaded that Heidegger's commentary on Hölderlin—which is at bottom what authorizes, retrospectively, the possibility of speaking of an "age of the poets"—is more concerned with the Mytheme than with the Poem (and that it is, to say it as clearly as possible, a forced attempt at *remythologization*), I would like to move against the flow of this commentary, as it were, in an attempt to survey its implications. These implications are, as is well known, indissociably philosophical and political, but they also touch on a certain poetology or on what we attempt to name, in a very fragile way, with the term *writing*, and thus also on what is at once affirmed and hidden in what Blanchot has referred to as the "exigency to write."

This assumes of course that a different light can be shed on Hölderlin, or that we will not prevent this text—and *all* of this text—from resonating in a different way.

As I said a moment ago, this is a work in progress. Here I will try to say something not so much about where it stands at the moment—like every work in progress, it stands nowhere—as about the direction it is taking, what is inspiring it, the suspicion from which it proceeds.

We may recall the way in which Adorno, in his essay "Parataxis," brings out the blunder, which was in any case intentional in the most heavy-handed way, committed by Heidegger in his commentary on "Andenken" ("Remembrance") from 1943. The passage, or rather passages, merit citation:

> The comments Heidegger appends, with visible discomfort, to the lines from "Andenken" ["Remembrance"] about the brown women of Bordeaux are of the same sort. "*The women*—Here this name still has the early sound that signifies the mistress and protectress. Now, however, the name is spoken solely with reference to the birth of essence in the poet. In a poem written shortly before his hymnic period and as part of the transition to it, Hölderlin said everything that can be known ('Gesang des Deutschen,' 11th stanza, IV, 130):
>
>> Den deutschen Frauen danket! sie haben uns
>> Der Götterbilder freundlichen Geist bewahrt.
>>
>> [Thank the German women! They have preserved
>> The friendly spirit of the gods' images for us.]
>
> [Heidegger continues:] The hymn 'Germanien' illuminates the poetic truth of these lines, which remained concealed from the poet himself. The German women rescue the manifestation of the gods so that it remains an event in history whose stay eludes the clutches of time-reckoning, which when in ascendancy can establish 'historical situations.' The German women rescue the arrival of the gods by placing it in the kindliness of a friendly light. They take away the fearsomeness of this event, whose frightening quality leads people astray into excess, whether in concretizing the divine nature and its loci or in grasping their essence. The preservation of this arrival is the constant cooperative work of preparing the celebration. In the greeting in 'Andenken,' however, it is not the German women who are named but the 'braunen Frauen daselbst' ['the brown women there']."[8] The assertion, by no means substantiated, that the word "Frauen" [women] here still has the early—one might add, Schillerian—tone "that signifies the mistress and protectress," whereas on the contrary Hölderlin's lines are enraptured with the erotic *imago* of the Mediterranean woman, allows Heidegger to pass unnoticed over to the praise of German women, of whom it is simply not a question in the poem being explicated. They are dragged in by the hair.[9]

Adorno's remark, or rather his reproach, is obviously correct inasmuch as it speaks plainly of erotic fascination, and inasmuch as it thus contradicts Heidegger's emphatic and pious commentary—to say nothing of its very weighty political overdetermination—which lends itself so poorly to the diction proper to this poem, concerned as it is with "sobriety." From the work of Dieter Henrich, Pierre Bertaux, and especially Jean-Pierre Lefebvre, we know to what extent Hölderlin's poetry becomes, after his return from Bordeaux, rigorously *literal*. What characterizes his poetry at that time, a poetry that is already becoming more and more fragmentary and disarticulated—and more and more enigmatic—is its extreme precision, its disarmed clarity, through which one begins to see emerge what Benjamin called "the naked rock of language."[10] This is so whether it is a question of things or human beings, place names or names in general, or even concepts (that is at least what Adorno tries to show). As Jean-Pierre Lefebvre says, using a common French expression: "After his return from France, and perhaps despite certain appearances, Hölderlin *calls a cat a cat*. When he evokes his stay abroad, for example, he does so with an almost photographic precision—or, to put the matter differently, he has become extraordinarily prosaic."[11] (I will come back to this last category in a moment.) "Andenken" speaks in reality, that is concretely, of Bordeaux, although I rather doubt that it is necessary to understand "the real" and "the concrete" in their speculative sense, as Adorno too plainly and simply does. And if it is—and especially *was*—important to recall that a poem, as a *poem,* in its "poetized" element or in its "*dictamen*" (if one can thus translate what Benjamin, and later Heidegger, called *das Gedichtete*),[12] is not limited to evoking "lived experiences" or relating the story or rendering an account of a journey or a visit—a demonstration to which Heidegger restricts himself (alas!) at the beginning of his commentary—it is also necessary (and *was* necessary) to speak with a singular bad faith and with very precise intentions, in order to deny *a priori* what I will call the (in fact rather desperate) sense of *reality* in the late Hölderlin. Or, if you prefer: his "urgent demand [*exigence*] for truth."

I will cite the incriminated stanza, and a translation that, to my knowledge, is the only one of the half dozen in existence that does not "over-poetize" the original and which restores it to its disarming, and disarmed, simplicity[13] (again I use this term which punctuates the last poems, as do words such as "naked" or other equivalents).

Noch denket das mir wohl und wie
Die breiten Gipfel neiget
Der Ulmwald, über die Mühl',
Im Hofe aber wächset ein Feigenbaum.
An Feiertagen gehn
Die braunen Frauen daselbst
Auf seidnen Boden,
Zur Märzenzeit,
Wenn gleich ist Nacht und Tag,
Und über langsamen Stegen,
Von goldenen Träumen schwer,
Einwiegende Lüfte ziehen.

Still I remember this, and how
The elm wood inclines
Its wide crests over the mill,
But in the courtyard a fig-tree grows.
But on holidays walk
The brown women in that place
On a silken floor,
In the month of March,
When night and day are equal,
And over slow walkways,
Heavy with golden dreams,
Lulling breezes drift.

There is not only an astonishing topographical precision here, as there is also in the first strophe (which is a "view" of Lormont) or in the last (which evokes a "view" of the Ambès headland). But if Adorno could not have known, we do know this today: the mill, located in fact in Lormont (on the opposite bank of the Garonne, therefore across from Bordeaux), was the space for a sort of cabaret where people came to dance on Sundays and, if not exactly a house of pleasure, in the years of the Directoire and the Consulate, at least a place for parties. In this sense Adorno is on the mark, quite simply because he knows to what extent Heidegger is avoiding the reality that Hölderlin, for his part, was at great pains to rejoin.

What is strange is that at the moment when he is correcting Heidegger in this way, Adorno suddenly shows himself to be very timid with regard to the obvious political importance of the lines he has just cited. Now there is no need to recall complacently (in the manner of Victor Farías) Elfriede Heidegger's "Thoughts of a Mother"; the German woman is an official *topos* of those years, and whatever theologico-political dimension Heidegger may confer on it (which is in fact immeasurable), the mere repetition of the theme, especially in such a ridiculously irrelevant manner, *also* amounts to a renewal or an approval of the *topos*. Indeed, Adorno adds, "Clearly, in 1943, when the philosophical commentator was working with 'Andenken,' he must have feared even the appearance of French women as something subversive; but even afterward he changed nothing in this bizarre excursus. Heidegger returns to the pragmatic content of the poem cautiously and shamefacedly, confessing that it is not the German but rather 'the brown women there' who are named."[14] There is no doubt that in the rest of his treatment Adorno is much more virulent toward Heidegger, never missing an opportunity to point out the latter's profound adherence to what Adorno calls, classically, "German ideology."[15] In this vein, one could also consider that "Parataxis" sets forth in an abridged form the essential points of the demonstration developed at length, around the same time, in *The Jargon of Authenticity*.[16] It would seem that here, however, despite the enormity of Heidegger's claims, Adorno does not strike as hard as he might.

Just exactly what is happening?

✠ ✠ ✠   What is happening—permit me to formulate the hypothesis in this way; it is not simply a matter of word play—is that something is happening with what happens in the exigency that the late Hölderlin discovers and to which he tries desperately to respond. The *agon* between Adorno and Heidegger is fought on the very site where Hölderlin pronounces the injunction which, on the eve of his departure for Bordeaux, abruptly acquires the force of law: *Aber das eigene muss so gut gelernt seyn, wie das Fremde* (letter to Böhlendorf of 4 December 1801).[17] Which I would transcribe in the following manner: "But what is one's own [*le propre*] must be learned [*il faut l'apprendre*] as well as the foreign." And which I will let resonate—since the analogy, stylistic and otherwise, is so constant in Adorno's essay—with this marginal note found in the score of Beethoven's 16th (and last) string quartet: *Muss es sein?—Es muss sein.* (Must it be?—It must be.)—What is played out with the "brown women" is the entire question of the relation between the proper and the foreign, the proximate and the distant. I would say also, taking up a lexicon that Lacan had himself transcribed from Heidegger: between the real and the nothing, or between the concrete and the thing. This question functions according to the logic of an augmentation determined by an infinitely inverse relation, at work for example in the Heideggerian concept of *Ent-fernung* (dis-stancing)[18] that I took the risk of naming, with reference to Hölderlin's interpretation of the tragic, a "hyperbologic,"[19] and according to which, if we may remain with these simple words: the closer it is, the farther away it is—and conversely. This logic involves a suspension of the dialectic itself. Adorno, in his way, that is, according to his own peculiar fidelity, knew this very well. Indeed, after the passage on the "brown women," he continues with the following, in which one sees very well that while he casts doubt on any usage of the (now stained) term "fatherland," not only does he not object to the thematic of the proximate and the proper, he even emphasizes its abyssal or—as he puts it in the language of "messianism"—utopian character:

> Basing himself both on statements by Hölderlin and on titles of poems, Beissner called the late hymns "die vaterländische Gesänge" ["Songs of the Fatherland"]. To have reservations about what Beissner did is not to have doubts about its philological justification. In the hundred and fifty years since these poems were written, however, the word *Vaterland* itself has changed for the worse; it has lost the innocence that still accompanied it in Keller's lines "Ich weiss in meinem Vaterland / Noch manchen Berg, O Liebe" ["I know many a mountain in my fatherland, O love"]. Love of what is close at hand and nostalgia for the warmth of childhood have developed into something exclusionary, into hatred for the other, and the word cannot be wiped clean of this. It has become permeated with a nationalism of which there is no trace whatsoever in Hölderlin. The right-wing German cult of Hölderlin has used his concept of what belongs to the fatherland in a distorted way, as though it were concerned with their idol and not with the felicitous balance between the total and

the particular. Hölderlin himself had already noted what later became evident in the word: "Verbotene Frucht, wie der Lorbeer, aber ist / am meisten das Vaterland" ["The fatherland is mostly, however, / Like the laurel, forbidden fruit"]. The continuation, "Die aber kost' / Ein jeder zuletzt" ["But each one tastes it in the end"], does not prescribe a plan for the poet so much as envision the utopia in which love of what is close at hand would be freed from all enmity.[20]

I have no intention of minimizing the disagreement that sets Adorno in opposition to Heidegger. Adorno's hostility is overt, and, moreover, it is never belied. As for the severity of the grievances, all of which are very fitting, it is without appeal. And these grievances are not only political (especially in terms of the political use of Hölderlin, an oblique example of which criticism we just saw) or philosophical (the question of being, in Adorno's eyes, is strictly inconsistent). They are equally, and I would say more seriously, aesthetic (the hyper-aestheticization of Hölderlin betrays the absence of all aesthetic sense) and above all hermeneutical and poetological: Heidegger may well deal with the concept of the poetized or the *dictamen*; he nevertheless knows nothing of the complex (or, in Adorno's sense, dialectical) relation between form, content, and the "truth content" (*Wahrheitsgehalt*: Benjamin's concept), and he has no understanding of what is "specifically poetic":[21] consequently he treats only the gnomic element, the pronouncements and maxims. And this, of course, in the most arbitrary manner possible (it is a thought authorized by nothing but itself for the purpose of decreeing its kinship, or its brotherhood, with Hölderlin's "poetic saying.")

One cannot therefore proceed as though this implacable critique did not exist.

At the same time, neither can one fail to notice the extent to which Adorno is attentive to what underlies Heidegger's commentary. One sign of this is given by a single phrase: "Poems and philosophy have the same aim: the *Wahrheitsgehalt* [truth content]."[22] The *Wahrheitsgehalt*, it is true, is not the same thing as *alētheia,* and Adorno has nothing but contempt for Heidegger's grandiloquent *Denken und Dichten* (thinking and poetizing). But this means indeed that he intends to do battle on the same terrain and that he never calls into question the absolutely privileged relation of (great) poetry to philosophy—a relation that, moreover, he goes out of his way to justify, over and against the philologists, at the beginning of his essay. Thus, in the most paradoxical manner, a strange complicity is established. I would call it an infinitely reticent complicity. It is discernible in the following passage (among others):

> Certainly, a number of Hölderlin's lines are suited to Heidegger's commentaries; ultimately, they are products of the same philhellenic-philosophical tradition. There is a mythic layer inherent in the substance of Hölderlin's work, as in any genuine demythologization. One cannot simply charge Heidegger with arbitrariness. Since the interpretation of poetry bears upon what was not said, one cannot hold against the interpretation the fact that it was not said in the poem. But one can demonstrate that what Hölderlin does not say is not what Heidegger extrapolates. When Heidegger reads the words, "Schwer verlässt, / Was nahe dem Ursprung wohnet, den Ort" ["For that which dwells / Near to its origin hardly will leave the place"], he may rejoice in both the pathos of the origin and the praise of immobility. But the strange line, "Ich aber will dem Kaukasos zu!" ["But I am bound for the Caucasus!"], which breaks in *fortissimo,* in the spirit of the dialectic—and that of Beethoven's *Eroica*—is not compatible with that kind of mood.[23]

A conflict of interpretations, then. But when I speak of an infinitely reticent complicity—which in the end can go as far as anger—I wish to emphasize *both* the complicity *and* the reticence, each one continually arising out of the other.

The complicity takes shape, as we just saw, in terms of Hölderlin's relation to philosophy, that is, to the speculative idealism he helped to construct, even though in a certain sense he also paralyzed it in advance. Whereas Heidegger remains in the end relatively prudent (at least in what he *wrote*), Adorno, in his obstinate but *faulty* fidelity to Hegel (and this is what is at stake in the "negative dialectic"), seeks in every way to establish a kinship between Hölderlin and the Hegelian dialectic, even if for Adorno this dialectic is without reconciliation. Thus he remarks, for example, on the famous note in the commentary on "Andenken" in which Heidegger sidesteps the necessity for a philosophical interpretation of one of the last reworkings of the final strophe of "Brot und

Wein": "For the spirit is not at home / in the beginning, at the source. The homeland consumes it. / The spirit loves the colony, and a bold forgetting." Adorno writes:

> Jesuitically, Heidegger makes his peace with Hölderlin's stance on empirical reality by seeming to leave unanswered the question of the relevance of the historico-philosophical tradition from which Hölderlin emerged, while suggesting that Hölderlin's relationship to that tradition is irrelevant to the poetized element [*fürs Gedichtete*]: "To what extent the law of historicity poetized [*gedichtete*] in these lines can be derived from the principle of unconditioned subjectivity in the German absolute metaphysics of Schelling and Hegel, in terms of which spirit's abiding-with-itself already requires spirit's return to itself, and the latter in turn requires its being-outside-itself—to what extent such a reference to metaphysics, even if it discovers 'historically accurate' relationships, illuminates the poetic law or obscures it instead, is presented only as a matter for subsequent reflection."[24]
>
> [Adorno comments:] Although Hölderlin cannot be dissolved into relationships within so-called intellectual history, nor the substance [*Gehalt*] of his work naively reduced to philosophical ideas, still he cannot be removed from the collective contexts in which his work took shape and with which it communicates, down to the very cells of its language.[25]

And from there, by means of an oblique reference to what Hölderlin might one day have called the "communism of spirits," Adorno goes on to demonstrate the profound solidarity between Hölderlin and his "comrades," a solidarity that "extends into the form as well"; and he does this not at the level of the "conceptual apparatus" but in relation to the "fundamental experiences striving for expression in the medium of thought."[26] Hölderlin's fundamental experience, like that of Hegel, is the experience of the "historically finite" as a necessary moment of "the appearance of the absolute."[27] And this is what Heidegger's ontologization of history does not allow him to see. It is true that Adorno does not understand, or pretends not to understand, what the question of being might consist in. To say that it can be reduced to "a simple antithesis,"[28] even while citing some particular proposition of Heidegger ("Being is never a being"),[29] simply leaves one dumbfounded, so great is the misinterpretation evinced by the word *antithesis*. But at the same time, Adorno is not wrong to claim that Hölderlin and Hegel "were in agreement all the way down to explicit theorems, such as for example in the critique of Fichte's absolute 'I' . . ., a critique which was no doubt canonical for Hölderlin's transition, at the end of his work, to empirical particulars."[30] It is here, however, that beyond the surface hostility the complicity is formed, and the infinite reticence.

Just after remarking this fundamental solidarity between Hölderlin and Hegel, Adorno adds:

> Heidegger, for whose philosophy the relationship of the temporal and the essential is thematic under another name, doubtless sensed the depth of what Hölderlin shared with Hegel. This is why he devalued it so zealously. Through his all too ready use of the word "being" he obscures what he himself has seen. Hölderlin suggests that the historical is ur-historical, hence all the more crucial the more historical it is. By virtue of this experience, determinate beings attain a weight in the poetized element of Hölderlin's language that slips *a fortiori* through the meshes of Heidegger's interpretation. Just as for Hölderlin's kindred spirit Shelley, Hell is a city "much like London," and just as later the modernity of Paris is an archetype for Baudelaire, so Hölderlin sees correspondences between ideas and particular beings everywhere. What the language of those years called "the finite" must do is exactly what the metaphysics of Being hopes for in vain: to lead beyond the concept the names which the absolute lacks and in which alone it would be.[31]

To lead beyond the concept the names of which the absolute is *in default*. It is evident, in the very passion and precipitousness of Adorno's demonstration, that the difference with Hegel is in fact decided here: in the question of the *name* as beyond the *concept*. We are very close to the famous line in the elegy "Homecoming" that Heidegger used as one of the leitmotifs of his commentary, and with which moreover he entitled one of the last texts he wrote: *Es fehlen heilige Namen:* "Sacred (or holy) names are lacking [*font défaut*]." But at this precise point, where Heidegger engages in a remythologization—and Adorno perceived this very clearly: "Out of complicity with myth," he says, "Heidegger forces Hölderlin to bear witness for the latter, and he thereby prejudices the result by his method"[32]—Adorno, for his part, takes a completely different path. It is no doubt clear by now that, at bottom, both of them

attempt to pull Hölderlin away from the speculative dialectic. But I
would say, schematically, that while Heidegger's strategy with respect
to Hegel is to orient himself within a logic of the future anterior (and
absolutely anterior)—within a "return upstream"[33] as it was called by
the unhappy René Char, who was one of its last pitiful victims—Adorno
attempts rather to wage the war of the modern. With the notion that
Hölderlin was in truth the first really to have led the way.

A moment ago, the name of Baudelaire was heard to resonate, and it
was no doubt immediately understood under whose authority Adorno
places himself in his reading of Hölderlin. Everything in it, or almost
everything, proceeds from the striking and notorious essay by Benjamin, "Two Poems by Friedrich Hölderlin," written in the winter of
1914–15 and published for the first time in 1955, in a collection edited,
in fact, by Adorno.[34] I cannot demonstrate this here, but I would like to
argue that, all things considered, Adorno does little more than apply (by
extending them over the entirety of the oeuvre) the "methodological"
principles and the hermeneutic intuition that Benjamin had tested—in
an essay that in this case can certainly be seen as a precursor—on the
example of the late reworking, after the "return from France," of an
earlier poem.

One of the most strategically decisive concepts in Adorno's demonstration is the concept of "demythologization" (Entmythologisier-
ung)—which of course must not be confused with the slogan of the
Protestant theology inspired by Heidegger (or inspired in Heidegger
by Bultmann), but which, however, has very much to do with another
concept that Adorno began to construct around the same time, that
is, the concept of Entkunstung [literally: de-artification], and which, a
few years later, will become the master concept of Aesthetic Theory; it
is through this concept that Adorno will attempt to approach in one
movement the Hegelian and the Heideggerian interpretations of art.[35]
"Demythologization" is opposed, in an entirely explicit way, to the
Heideggerian determination of Dichtung as Sage (in which it is difficult not to recognize the German translation of the Greek muthos).
And the word is a manifest condensation of what Benjamin called,
in 1915, the Verlagerung des Mythologischen. (This has been translated

as the "setting down" or "deposing of the mythological.") The entire problematic of the sacred in Heidegger is delimited here in advance, and consequently—in connection with the latter's conception of the essence of *Dichtung*—so is that of the vocation or mission of the poet.

When Benjamin constructed his concept of the *dictamen*—a term that very clearly, and in the closest proximity, evokes the kinship of *dichten* and *dictare*,[36] while allowing the *il faut* of an exigency to resonate as well: Rousseau spoke of "the *dictamen* of my conscience"—he deduced it, as we know, from Goethe's notion of "content" (*Gehalt*). This is not content in the sense of that which is contained, but the "internal form," which Benjamin will identify with the *Wahrheitsgehalt*, the "truth-content." The content is the *dictamen*, that which in the poem emerges properly from the poetic, inasmuch as it designates at once the *task* of the poet—which is inferred from the poem itself (indeed, the first version of the poem studied by Benjamin is entitled "The Poet's Courage," *Dichtermut*)—and the presupposition of the poetry, that is, the intuitive-spiritual structure of the world to which the poem bears witness. The task is *die Aufgabe*, a duty, and another form of the *il faut*, located somewhere between rendering and abandoning, giving over and giving up: The task is quite simply the *courage of poetry*, in the double sense of the genitive. One could show that this is in reality the transcendental schema of poetry.

Benjamin states explicitly that the *dictamen* is a limit-concept, and that as such it maintains a double relation: with respect to the functional unity of the poem (the relation of the form and the content), whose necessary connection it expresses; and with respect to life, to the functional unity of life, which is contained in the idea of a task. The *dictamen* ensures the passage from the second to the first, from life to the poem. That is why the *dictamen* is not a stranger to the mythic, in the sense in which, for example, on the basis of an ancient mimetology that had been reactivated by the romantics and by Nietzsche (but by Hölderlin as well), Thomas Mann was able to speak of "life in the myth" in order thus to designate, in sum, an ethics of exemplarity.[37] And this was indeed, I believe, the very pain of Hölderlin. But the mythic is not the myth, neither in the sense of this or that particular myth, nor in the sense of the essential unity of myths. The latter is rather the mytho-logical and is precisely what it is necessary to "set down" or "depose." The mythic is, on the contrary, the internal tension and contradiction of the mythical elements—that in which, in effect, Hölderlin did not cease to struggle. And in the end it is the collapse of myth, or of the mythological.

Benjamin's analysis of the two versions of the poem is intensely difficult. It would be necessary to follow it step by step. Despite many attempts at exegesis, among which I count definitively the use made of it by Adorno, it retains a certain mystery. As for myself, unable to see how I could even conceive of attempting to penetrate it here, I would like simply to recall, in its enigmatic suspension, Benjamin's (inconclusive) conclusion:

> The contemplation of the *dictamen,* however, leads not to myth but rather—in the greatest creations—only to mythic connections, which in the work of art are shaped into unique, unmythological, and unmythic forms that cannot be better understood by us.[38]

> But if there were words with which to grasp the relation between myth and the inner life from which the later poem sprang, it would be those of Hölderlin from a period still later than that of this poem: "Myths [*die Sagen, hoi muthoi*], which take leave [*sich entfernen*] of earth, / ... They return to mankind [*Sie kehren zu der Menschheit sich*]."[39]

There would thus be a law governing the *Ent-fernung* or dis-stancing of myth—a distancing that it would perhaps not be going too far to call categorical. This law would permit us to glimpse the appearance, in the greatest poems, of this nonmythological and nonmythic figure, which, it will be noticed, is a sheer oxymoron, since there is no *Gestalt* that is not by definition mythic or mythological. Every great poem would thus tend toward a figure that is absolutely paradoxical in that this figure would be sustained by nothing but the very lack and default of that which ought to support it. This is what I would like to call, according to the logic of the *il faut, la défaillance du mythe*: the failure of myth.

It is not by chance that a few lines further along, in the opening part of his "conclusion," Benjamin relates this failure of myth—which is thus conceived precisely in accordance with the *il faut* of the poem, that is, its *dictamen*—to the notion of "sobriety," to that *heilige Nüchternheit* (sacred sobriety).[40] And here perhaps the word *heilig* does not simply mean the "sacred" in the way that Heidegger wants at all cost to hear it, if only because it defines what is proper to "Hesperia," that is, the destiny of modern man and modern art, turned aside or away in the manner of Oedipus, "like a traitor, but indeed in a way that is holy." This is how Benjamin reveals his proposed interpretation of what Hölderlin called the proper, or the "nationell." I believe that it goes far beyond anything Heidegger was ever able to say about the matter:

> In the course of this investigation, the word "sobriety" was deliberately avoided, a word that might often have served for purposes of characterization. Only now shall Hölderlin's phrase "sacredly sober" be uttered, now that its understanding has been determined. Others have noted that these words exhibit the tendency of his later creations. They arise from the inner certainty with which those works stand in his own spiritual life, in which sobriety now is allowed, is demanded, because this life is in itself sacred, standing—beyond all elevation—in the sublime [*jenseits aller Erhebung im Erhabenen*]. Is this life still that of Hellenism? This is as little the case here as it is that a pure work of art could ever be that of a people; and as little the case, too, that it could be that of an individual, or anything other than this proper element which we find in the *dictamen*.[41]

Such statements are certainly of a sort to allow Adorno (and a few others after him) to call into question, with respect to the contents of the poems, Heidegger's indeed painfully nationalist variations on the "fatherland" as the truth of the "colony" (or the "return" as the truth of "exile"). Or the interpretation of "Andenken," concerned entirely with reversing the course of what is said (from Bordeaux to Nürtingen and from Nürtingen to Indus, in accordance with the thematic of the rivers flowing back toward their source), while the Garonne, which in fact flows in reverse at each tide, is the promise of a crossing, borne by the northeasterly or the alizé, leading all the way to the West Indies (the Windward Islands); Hölderlin says in a more lapidary fashion: "zu Indiern," to Indians. (On this point, as on many others, Jean-Pierre Lefebvre's demonstration is perfectly convincing.)

But Benjamin's argument has another dimension. It goes not only beyond the register of "empirical particulars" or "concrete objects," but also beyond that of the sublime considered, in the manner of Schiller, as a simple elevation toward ideality. It gestures, in other words, toward a completely other *simplicity* (which would be the very nakedness of finitude) insofar as it refers sobriety back to the "inner certainty" with which Hölderlin's poems "inhabit the very heart of his spiritual life" and when he says of this life that it is nothing "other than the proper element" of the *dictamen*.

We are touching here, at the point of myth's failure, on what I propose to call the *thing* [*la chose*], which is also the *cause* of the poem. I know of no emblematic formula for this "thing" more rigorously sober than the one found, again, in the first letter to Böhlendorf, at the point where Hölderlin wants to indicate what he understands as the *modern* tragic, "For this is the tragic for us: that, packed into some simple box [*Behälter*], we very quietly move away from the realm of the living, and not that—consumed in flames—we expiate the flames which we could not tame."[42] Such is the thing: a simple box, not to say a mere "container." Here, Hölderlin's writing would find its destination—but in the form of the modern destiny that consists in "wandering under the unthinkable"—as well as his response to the *dictamen: it is necessary to say the thing*, the abyss of the proper and the proximate.

I would like to end by touching on this in a few words.

It is not difficult to see that the point of myth's failure is situated at the very place that I will call, no doubt for lack of a better term, *dis-figuration*. Or, if I were to risk a translation: *Entgestaltung*.

By dis-figuration I mean every form of destruction or decomposition of the figure, or even, yet more simply, every form of rarefaction, disappearance or abandonment: everything that I placed at the outset under the sign of *literalization*. But it goes without saying that dis-figuration is not the suppression or, even less, the sublation (the *Aufhebung*) of the figure. To name the thing is not to render obsolete the idea, the concept or the essence, neither is it to declare them vain in the name of "the real" or "the concrete." It is rather to mark them, but as a hollow or as a negative, in the photographic sense of the term, as Jean-Pierre Lefebvre would say. To stay with the example of "Andenken," when Hölderlin says "Steg" (walkway), we may hear "Weg" or "Pfad" (path), as Heidegger does, without lessening in the least the enormous philo-sophico-poetic burden of the image (which would not be an image) of the path. But it may be preferable to understand "Steg" as a desperate allusion, from within the most precise renunciation, to "Weg," but where "Weg" could still of course be read as the figure, henceforth at its end and in the process of collapsing, that it was and probably remains in the very moment when Hölderlin addresses to it this last farewell gesture. Dis-figuration, if you will permit me to remain stubbornly with the lexicon that I took up at the beginning, is the very failure of the figure, which is to say the purest affirmation of its *il faut*. Put another way, dis-figuration is the retreat or withdrawal of the figure. Just as the retreat of the divine does not signify, for Hölderlin, the death of God or of the gods, neither does dis-figuration signify the pure and simple disappearance of the figure: It designates its becoming absent (because henceforth impossible), and it does so by way of what this becoming absent leaves as an ineffaceable trace.

Dis-figuration affects everything within the order of the *transport*, as Hölderlin says, in French, when he elaborates the so-called formal or structural conception of tragedy and introduces the important notion of the "caesura." It therefore affects at the same time everything within the order of the meta-phorical and the meta-physical: of "mythopoi-esis" and the speculative. Or in yet another possible formulation, ev-erything within the order of the name and the concept.

In reference to myth, it is clear that, at least for Hölderlin, the figure is first of all the name. The phrase from Adorno that I have already quoted—"To lead beyond the concept the names of which the abso-lute is in default"—gives a precise indication in this direction. And yet Adorno is the first to remark that in Hölderlin name and concept are not precisely distinguished. He cites this line from "Patmos": "For the wrath of the world is without concept, without name." The name stands in for the concept, at least insofar as the name stands in for the *Gestalt*, in the Hegelian sense, that is, as the concept of a finite moment that signs a missive from the absolute. But in *The Phenomenology of Spirit*, the *Gestalt* does not properly speaking carry a name; it remains conceptual: self-certainty, mastery and servitude, unhappy conscious-ness, etc. Even "Antigone" does not name a figure, that of *Sittlichkeit* (the ethical order), any more than does "Christ" when it is a question of revealed religion. The name would thus be aimed, as a consequence, at the (mythical) beyond of the concept. In order to designate this beyond, Adorno speaks in dialectical terms of a "non-conceptual synthesis," and we know that this expression conveys his definition of "great music." It is, he says, "the primal image for Hölderlin's late poetry, just as Hölderlin's idea of song [*Gesang*] can be rigorously applied to music." Adorno is evidently thinking of Beethoven, all the more in that he adds, by way of explanation, the following remark, which is transparent: "a liberated, outflowing nature that transcends itself precisely through having escaped from the spell of the domination of nature."[43] Now such a "non-conceptual synthesis" is likewise aimed at the name. We might recall the passage in "Music and Language: A Fragment," which opens the collection *Quasi una Fantasia,* in which Adorno makes music the equivalent, in the end, of what Benjamin called "pure language." "The language of music is quite different from the language of intentionality. It contains a theological dimension. What it has to say is simultaneously revealed and concealed. Its Idea is the divine Name which has been given shape. It is demythologized prayer, rid of efficacious magic. It is the human attempt, doomed as ever, to name the Name, not to communicate meanings."[44] And yet Adorno remarks that "in poetry, unlike music, non-conceptual synthesis turns against its medium," that is, against language that, for its part, is at once the possibility and the element of conceptual synthesis—such that in poetry, by the very fact of language, the nonconceptual synthesis becomes what Adorno calls a "constitutive dissociation."[45] By aiming at what music alone can aim at, the pure name, poetry becomes dislocated; and beyond syntax (that is, beyond what Adorno analyzes as the "paratactic" style of the late Hölderlin), this affects nomination itself. Just as there is a dissociation of syntax, which is intensified even further by the transposition of Greek prosody, there is also a "dissociation of names"—and even, at the limit, a "rupture of the name." Attempting to locate the greatest difference separating Hölderlin and Hegel, Adorno notes the following, the correctness of which seems indisputable: "The difference between the name and the absolute, which Hölderlin does not conceal and which runs through his work like an allegorical cleft, is the medium of his critique of the false life, in which the soul is not granted its divine right."[46] Contrary to what Heidegger wants to believe, the name, in Hölderlin, no longer names. It evokes, or rather signals, the lost or fractured possibility of naming. The greatest of Baudelaire's poems on Paris, and on the most aggressively modern Paris, begins with these words: "Andromache I think of you!"[47] But this is still a precise allusion to the mythical episode of the captivity of Andromache. In "Andenken," such de-nomination (*Entnennung*) is even more radical: aside from the place names (Bordeaux, Garonne, Dordogne) and the ethno-geographic mention of the Indians, the poem contains only a single proper name, that of Bellarmin, which designates no one—at least no one other than Hyperion's mute correspondent—and means nothing—except perhaps, in Jean-Pierre Lefebvre's hypothesis, "bello Arminius," a sort of Germanic *kaloskagathos*.[48] A calcination of the name: The figure, the *Gestalt,* is indeed there, but it presents itself (*stellt sich dar*) as the forever withdrawn or truncated secret of the name, as empty nomination. A few years later, Hölderlin will sign his name as Scardanelli.

That is why—I return to this point—it is correct to speak of *prosaism,* if what is meant by this is a writing that is not only, as Adorno says, "incommensurable with the poetry of ideas and with autobiographical poetry" (with lyricism as a genre that is subjective in a false or facile way), but that sees itself compelled—again a question of an imperative—to take leave of the hymn, to quit it. To say, like the Rimbaud of "A Season in Hell": "Adieu." A gesture that can be understood in French in many ways, but which resonates in German in this very beautiful word: *Abschied.*[49]

Speaking of the late hymns, Adorno says: "Pure language, whose idea they figure, would be a prose analogous to sacred texts." I am not convinced that the expression "sacred texts" is altogether fitting, even if "pure language," according to Benjamin, communicates nothing and is indeed the language that communicates itself as the fact that there is language—in which God, in default of a name, is designated. But the word "prose" is absolutely fitting. And I would say that it is all the more fitting in that it is precisely the word in which Heidegger's sacralization of the *dictamen* encounters its greatest obstacle. Let us refer again to the commentary on "Andenken," to the passage concerning the "brown women." Heidegger reads Hölderlin's line, *Die braunen Frauen daselbst,* literally: "The brown women in that place," or as is more generally translated, "The brown women there." And he comments:

> In order to keep the distance, in its distant presencing, in its nearness, the poet says *there too* (*daselbst*), which to the contemporary ear comes close to legal or commercial language.[50] But the poetic character of the greeting resounds so simply throughout the whole stanza that any suggestion of the "prosaic" melts away. Above all, the poet during this period is so little inclined to shrink from a word which is at first unpoetic and peculiar that he even listens especially for such a word. He knows that for the invisible to be as pure as it must be, it demands all the more decisively from the naming word that it be effaced in the strangeness of the image.[51]

One can say without exaggeration, so clearly and exemplarily is the entire lexicon and all the syntactic resources of Heidegger's commentary condensed into these few lines, that the denial of the "prosaic"— and the rescue of the image (the *Bild*)—is the surest and probably the only means of saving, by way of a *Rettung* [salvation or rescue] that has nothing to do with Benjamin's, the sacred (mythical) character of Hölderlin's supposed sermonizing. Heidegger's *Dichtung* is—decidedly wants to make itself—the absolute opposite of prose. By which the dialectic resists, more than one might think.

But "prose" should in fact be understood as another name for "sobriety."

In the last pages of his thesis on the concept of criticism in the Romantics, in order to explain that the philosophy of art outlined by the Romantics culminates in the conception of "the Idea of poetry as prose" (in Novalis, for example, who says that "poetry is the prose among the arts"), Benjamin lays out two conditions: One must be able to recognize in philosophy itself the hard core of Romanticism and the foundation of its literary theory; but one must also be able to perceive that the most secret center of Romanticism is not found in Romanticism—or, if you prefer, that Romanticism does not have its center within itself. And he writes these lines, which even now are astounding:

From this point of view, one spirit moves into the wider circle, not to say into its center—a spirit who cannot be comprehended merely in his quality as a "poet" in the modern sense of the word (however high this must be reckoned), and whose relationship to the Romantic school, within the history of ideas, remains unclear if his particular philosophical identity with this school is not considered. This spirit is Hölderlin, and the thesis that establishes his philosophical relation to the Romantics is the principle of the sobriety of art. This principle is the essentially quite new and still incalculably influential leading idea of the Romantic philosophy of art; what is perhaps the greatest epoch in the West's philosophy of art is distinguished by this basic notion.[52]

And a little later, "in order to prepare the way for understanding the less clear statements of Friedrich Schlegel and Novalis," Benjamin cites at length the opening passages of Hölderlin's "Remarks," concerning the *mēchanē* [devices] of the ancients and the necessary calculation, "also among us," of rules.[53] It may not be sufficient to indicate, as Heidegger does again in *The Principle of Reason,* that calculation for Hölderlin should not be understood "in a quantitative and mechanical, or, let us say, a mathematical mode," even though this is after all somewhat obvious. And yet it is necessary to consider that it is indeed a question of calculation. And that such a calculation is the very condition of sobriety.

One can—*one must*—suppose that "Andenken" is thus calculated, according to the truth—*in default*—of poetry as prose. A sober poem, it would say the very failure of poetry, that is, precisely that which responds to the exigency to write, to the *il faut.* It would say this in its last line, whose enigma so many commentaries have failed to unravel: "Was bleibet aber, stiften die Dichter"—"But what remains, is founded by the poets"—or rather, I believe, is *instituted* by them.

CHAPTER 3

❦ ❦ ❦   The Courage of Poetry

That, after the brief period of manic activity in 1933–34 had passed, Heidegger's entire political preaching is essentially to be sought in his discourse on poetry—and particularly on Hölderlin—is not something that any of us has invented. He says this himself.

In a transitional passage from the course taught during the winter semester of 1934–35, entitled *Hölderlins Hymnen: "Germanien" und "Der Rhein"* (Hölderlin's Hymns: "Germania" and "The Rhine")—one of the first courses he gave after resigning from the rectorship—we read, as a reminder of the "task of the course" (*die Aufgabe der Vorlesung*), the following, which is perfectly clear:

> The goal of this course remains to recreate finally in our historial Dasein a space and a site for what poetry is. That can happen only when we bring ourselves into the sphere of power [*Machtbereich*] of an effective poetry and open ourselves to its effectivity. Why is Hölderlin's poetry chosen for this? This choice is no random selection from whatever poets are at hand. This choice is a historical decision. Let us name three of its essential grounds: 1) Hölderlin is the poet of poets and of poetry; 2) Conjoined to this, Hölderlin is the poet of the Germans; 3) Since Hölderlin is this in a concealed and difficult way, poet of poets as poet of the Germans, he has therefore not yet become a power in the history of our people. Since he is not yet that power, he must become it. To contribute to this is "politics" in the highest and most authentic sense, so much so that whoever effects anything here has no need to talk of the "political."[1]

(An incidental remark: You will have noticed that Heidegger presents here in a "decrypted" form the message that the Rome lecture from about two years later, "Hölderlin and the Essence of Poetry," will work hard to encode in a way that is simultaneously very canny and very crude, notably through the suppression of the signifier "the

Germans." As if at bottom, in a foreign country, and yet in "allied" territory, Heidegger had obscurely prepared his future reception, especially his French reception. And indeed, you are not unaware of the consequences, including those for French poetry, of Henry Corbin's 1938 translation of this lecture.[2] But that is another question.)

On the other hand, that this sort of call for a " 'politics' in the highest and most proper sense" (the word *politics*, it must be noted, is always, even here, given in quotes), beyond its patent "nationalism," takes the precise form of the theologico-political—this is something that Heidegger of course never said. He would even have firmly denied it. But it is also the case that no one, with very few exceptions, has noticed this. And yet it is no less clear.

I will give only one example, the one that presents itself most immediately. It is from the "Preliminary Remark" to the same lecture course—perhaps written (for the most part) after the fact, but that is neither very certain nor of any great interest. It bears the sober title "Hölderlin." I quote:

> He must remain silent for a long time yet, especially now that "interest" in him is beginning to stir and "literary history" is searching for new "themes." One writes now on "Hölderlin and his gods." That is indeed the most extreme misinterpretation, through which this poet, who only now stands before the Germans in their future, is definitively pushed aside into a complete lack of effectivity, under the pretext that one is finally doing him "justice." As if his work needed justice, especially from the poor judges found everywhere today. One handles Hölderlin "historically" and fails to recognize this one essential thing, that his work, which is still without its time and space, has already overcome [*überwunden*] our historicizing activity and founded [*gegründet*] the commencement of another history, the history that arises with the struggle [*Kampf*] in which the flight or the arrival of the god will be decided.[3]

(Allow me to make a second incidental remark here: Regardless of when this note may have been written—in any case it sanctions, in a very charged language, the carefully prepared and deliberate publication of a 1934 course with which it harmonizes perfectly—one thing is certain: up to his testamentary interview granted in 1966 to the editors of *Der Spiegel*, Heidegger will change practically nothing in the discourse he began to proffer at the moment of his "withdrawal" from National Socialism. As a reminder, I will recall his 1966 declaration: "Only a god can save us now. The sole possibility that is left for us is to prepare a sort of readiness, in thinking and poetry, for the appearance of the god or for the absence of the god in the time of decline [*Untergang*]; if we decline, let it be in the face of the absent god."[4] Let us pass over the very dated pathos of decline, or, if you prefer, the obsession with nihilism. It is nonetheless in declarations such as this that we find confirmed what I do not believe it exaggerated to call the theologico-political. It turns out to have been particularly tenacious in Heidegger; and we must indeed understand that if "actually existing National Socialism" was in his eyes merely "politics," that is because it was lacking not only an authentic sense of the *polis* (understood as the *Da* of *Sein*), but also a theology, that is, as we have already seen, a notion of the essence of art and of the only chance for "founding the beginning of another history.")

I will not enter here into a consideration of the complex and cunning relations that Heidegger maintains with theology, a word that, moreover, he does not repudiate. I am using the word *theology* in its simplest sense: the discourse on the divine. And so that things will be perfectly clear, I will quote the text that is probably the most explicit in this respect; it is from the "Letter on 'Humanism'" (1946), in which Heidegger attempts to define an "ethics" prior to ethics, that is, an "ethics" responding or corresponding to what is no longer even called "ontology"—for now I will call it, for lack of a better term, an archiethics—and in which he relies upon the Hölderlinian motifs of the homeland (*die Heimat*) or Germanness (*das Deutsche*). Here is the text (and do not forget that, at the time, this discourse was also an attempt to clear his name):

> "German" is not spoken to the world so that the world might be reformed through the German essence; rather, it is spoken to the Germans so that from a destinal belongingness to other peoples they might become world-historical along with them. [...] The homeland of this historical dwelling is nearness to being.
>
> In such nearness, if at all, a decision may be made as to whether and how God and the gods withhold their presence and the night remains,

whether and how the day of the holy dawns, whether and how in the upsurgence of the holy an apparition of God and the gods can begin anew. But the holy, which alone is the essential sphere of divinity, which in turn alone affords a dimension for the gods and for God, comes to radiant appearance only when being itself beforehand and after extensive preparation has been cleared and is experienced in its truth. Only thus does the overcoming (*Überwindung*) of homelessness begin from being, a homelessness in which not only human beings but the essence of the human being wanders aimlessly about.[5]

In 1934 Heidegger spoke to his students about the task of his teaching. This involved an injunction. We see that such a task was already nothing other than the "task of thinking" insofar as, at the "end of philosophy," this latter task accords with the one it assumes to have been that of poetry, that is, of Hölderlin: to prepare the coming—or to announce the turning away—of the god and of the gods. Face to face with nihilism, in a more radical sense than the one expressed in Nietzsche's "God is dead," which nonetheless subtended—it must be remembered—the entire engagement of the Rectoral Address. Task of thinking, task of poetry: an archi-ethics of this sort would have governed Heidegger's theologico-political preaching.

If this fundamental hypothesis is correct, I would like, then, to put forth a few propositions—in the somewhat lapidary form of a simple reminder. There are five:

1. The theologico-political is obviously supported only by a theologico-poetics (I hazard this term, here too for lack of a better one). It is the Hölderlinian "preaching" that authorizes the "political" preaching of the 1930s (and later), but we must understand: on the one hand, that this "preaching" (of Hölderlin, though I doubt that in the end it was one) thus has authority only because it lacks authority and because nothing and no one authorizes it (it is not a god that, as in the incipit of ancient poetry, dictates the Poem; it is on the contrary the "default of god" that "helps," that is, that makes the Poem possible, at the limit of the possible); and, on the other hand, that this authority is authority only because it is at the same time madness (the "protective night of the gods") that has sanctioned the impossible possibility of the Poem,

and this Poem has still not been heard or understood (which, moreover, is why the Germans are in a position of indebtedness with regard to Hölderlin).

The theologico-political of the ancients depends on the notion that—as the *Introduction to Metaphysics* (1935) affirms by recalling (without citing) Herodotus—it was Homer, under the injunction of the Muse, who "gave to Greece its gods." The theologico-political of the moderns is what suspends the poem in the announcement—the gospel—of the coming or the withdrawal of the gods.

2. The political, in the expression "theologico-political," is what touches on the national, or more precisely, as Hölderlin spelled this term, on the "nationell." That is, on the people. Heidegger, in the "Letter on 'Humanism'" (that is, in 1946 . . .), may well credit Marx with having experienced modern man's essential homelessness through the concept of alienation (the intuition is worth considering: Marx is not so far removed from Hölderlin, mass migrations organized by "industry" are a fact, and it is indeed a matter, in both cases, of an *alienation*), he nonetheless repudiates—and always will—both internationalism and nationalism alike, as figures of unconditioned subjectivity. And by this we should understand their doctrines as well as (*a fortiori*) their ideologies. Just before the passage from the "Letter on 'Humanism'" that I recalled a moment ago—and just after mentioning Nietzsche, who had himself undergone the experience of this homelessness and had "definitively closed off every way out" because he remained a prisoner of the "overturning of metaphysics"—Heidegger writes, "On the other hand, when Hölderlin composes 'Homecoming,' he is concerned that his 'countrymen' find their essence. He does not at all seek that essence in an egoism of his people. He sees it rather in the context of a belongingness to the destiny of the West. But even the West is not thought regionally as the Occident in contrast to the Orient, nor merely as Europe, but rather world-historically [*weltgeschichtlich*] out of nearness to the origin."[6]

Nevertheless, this same problematic concerning *Heimatlosigkeit* (homelessness or "uprootedness," to use the term favored by the conservative revolution, precisely in opposition to Marx's "alienation," *Entfremdung*) inevitably leads in the 1930s to a displacement of the

Kantian question (in a style that is indissociably *Aufklärer* and metaphysical) "What is man?" in favor of this other question: "Who are we?" And this means, no less inevitably: "Who are we, we Germans?" And one possible response is this, for example: the "philosophical people par excellence"; or: the "people of thinkers and poets." In short, the "metaphysical people."[7]

3. The theologico-political, in turn, is supported by a call to myth. I have already tried to show this elsewhere, so I will not insist on it here.[8] This thesis marks my opposition, friendly but firm, to one proposed by Alain Badiou.[9] I do not contest the notion of a suturing of philosophy, since Hegel, to one or another of its generic conditions. I am simply saying that in Heidegger this suturing occurs not with the Poem but with the Mytheme. The remark applies to the entirety of the great (German) metaphysical tradition since its Romantic *envoi* by the Schlegels, certainly, but especially by Schelling—who was a friend of Hölderlin, as we know. The Heideggerian apprehension of poetry is overdetermined by speculative Romanticism: That is indeed why poetry (*Dichtung*) is defined in its essence as language, *die Sprache*—or why language (and this amounts to the same) is defined as the originary poetry (*Urdichtung*) of a people—and, finally, why the latter in turn is defined in its essence as *die Sage: ho muthos*. Not the *Heldensaga*, the heroic legend, as Heidegger will specify in the 1950s: but the *muthein* that, in its indistinct difference from *legein* (the gathering, as language, of the "there is"), is alone capable of pronouncing divine places and names. In any case, *Dichtung*, like *logos* in its Aristotelian-phenomenological definition, is apophantic: *dichten*, by way of the high German *thîton* and the Latin *dictare*, goes back to the Greek *deiknumi*: to show, to designate, to make appear. Every sign (*Zeichen*) is a showing (*Zeigen*), that is, a naming (*Nennen*), which alone makes anything be. These sequences are well known, and the fact that when it comes to language Heidegger could refer to Herder and to Humboldt is in no way a matter of indifference.

4. Politics, in the sense in which Heidegger understood it without wanting to hear anything about it (always the quotation marks . . .), was nonetheless organically bound up in the 1930s with National Socialism—with fascism, bringing with it all the compromises we are

aware of or can easily imagine. Despite his disavowals, his half-avowals, or his lies, Heidegger was never really able to defend himself against this accusation. So if there is a *politics* for Heidegger during those years—and I maintain that there is one, inscribed, well beyond the "ordinary" compromise, in the texts themselves, explicitly or not—I would readily argue that it issued from what I will call (once again, for lack of a better term) an *archi-fascism*. Such an archi-fascism has nothing to do with the sur-fascism with which Breton, around 1934, thought himself clever enough to reproach Bataille. On the other hand, it has everything to do with the terrible judgment, pronounced all the more authoritatively for its timidity, spoken by Benjamin when, during a meeting of the College of Sociology at which Bataille had spoken on the sacred, he whispered in Klossowski's ear: "At bottom, you're working for the fascists." The logic of the *archi*, as Benjamin well knew, is absolutely formidable. And in this light, it is clear that Heidegger's discourse against "real fascism" had no other ambition, in reality, than to liberate the *truth* of fascism.

5. Alloyed with the theologico-poetic, under the conditions that we have seen, the theologico-political assigns to poetry a mission, in what is ultimately the most banal sense given to this word since the Romantics. This mission, as we have seen, is a struggle. But if this struggle is absolutely necessary in Heidegger's view, that is because there is a danger. In Rome in 1936, Heidegger condenses his 1934 course into five leitmotifs taken from Hölderlin's corpus; he quotes part of a prose fragment, placed for the moment in opposition to a declaration on the "innocence" of poetry, saying that language (*die Sprache*) is "the most dangerous of all goods." He proposes this commentary that, for its part, dispenses with all commentary, "But in what sense is language 'the most dangerous good'? It is the danger of all dangers because it first creates the possibility of a danger. Danger is the threat that beings pose to being itself. But it is only by virtue of language at all that man is exposed to something manifest; *beings* which press upon him and inflame him in his existence [*in seinem Dasein*], or *nonbeings* which deceive and disappoint him. Language first creates the manifest place of this threat to being, and the confusion and thus the possibility even of the loss of being, that is—danger."[10] And a little later he adds,

"Language gives expression to what is most pure and most concealed, as well as to what is confused and common. Indeed, even the essential word, if it is to be understood and so become the common possession of all, must make itself common. Accordingly, it is said in another of Hölderlin's fragments: "You spoke to the divinity, but this you have forgotten, that the first-fruits are not for mortals, that they belong to the gods. The fruit must first become more common, more everyday, then it will be the mortals' own."[11]

Heidegger glosses this quote in the following way: "The pure and the common both form in the same way a said." *Ein Gesagtes, eine Sage*: a myth.

We can easily deduce at least three things from this text. First, faced with the danger itself, danger in its essence (a threat that weighs on being), an archi-ethical quality is assumed and demanded of poetry: courage. Moreover, it is probably the only archi-ethical quality that one can discern in the Heideggerian discourse of the 1930s: What I am trying to call here the archi-ethical consists purely and simply in the experience of courage. Second, since every "ontological" danger is also, and necessarily, a historial danger—and the historial is, if you will, the political without quotation marks—a responsibility is given to poetry as well as to the thought that responds for it. This responsibility can be called transcendental in that the possibility of a history for a people depends on it alone. (And we could show that in a certain way this amounts to saying that courage lies in decision.) In the commentary on Hölderlin, the entire question is to know whether the Germans are capable of entering into history, and of opening a history: of becoming the Germans, the way the Greeks, with the unheard-of courage attested to in tragedy, became the Greeks. Finally, one obvious consequence is that the poet is defined as a *hero*, in the sense given to this word in section 74 of *Being and Time*, when it is said that historial *Dasein* (the people) must choose its heroes for itself in the tradition. In a direct lineage from Nietzsche's interpretation of history and from the ancient *agon*, the poet is more than a model, he is an *example*. Or, in the terminology of the Moderns, present in both Heidegger and Nietzsche, he is a figure, a *Gestalt*. Heidegger, who will violently refuse any figure derived from Nietzscheanism—from Zarathustra himself to Rilke's Angel and even, although indeed this is much later, Jünger's Worker—will nonetheless have accepted, and more than accepted, the figure of the hero of poetry, the demi-god, the mediator and intercessor between the gods and men, the immortals and the mortals: the one who, says Hölderlin (or at least a certain Hölderlin), takes hold of the signs of the divine, at the height of danger—under the immediate threat of being destroyed by lightning—in order to transmit them in a veiled form to the people. (The second part of the 1934 course, on the hymn "Germania," develops this motif at length; but it is constant in Heidegger.)

I resigned myself to recalling these points only in order to introduce the real subject of my paper this evening. I will present its major features in outline here, but only in outline, since, as you will see in a moment, it is obvious that much more detailed analyses would be necessary to do justice to the question that I would like to raise.

It so happens that exactly twenty years before Heidegger's initial (and initiating) commentary, Hölderlin and, in Hölderlin, the same motif of courage, had been the occasion for an interpretive gesture that was, so to speak, the inverse of Heidegger's. But not the complete inverse, which, I believe, has great consequences.

I am referring here to Benjamin's famous essay, written in the winter of 1914–15, entitled "Two Poems by Friedrich Hölderlin."[12] As you know, this text remained unpublished until 1955, when Adorno and Scholem presented the first collection of Benjamin's scattered essays. In 1936, Heidegger obviously could not have been aware of it. But at the same time my purpose is not to "compare" the two interpretations, which could be of only very limited interest. In evoking this text, it is rather a question of taking the measure of an epoch (with which we are far from finished) and of the philosophical questioning that subtends it: Our politics, and not only our politics, still depend on it.

A brief presentation of this text will be necessary here. It is a study of two versions of a single poem—a poem that in reality exists in three versions, but Benjamin deliberately neglects the intermediate version—the second (and final) of which, most certainly written after Hölderlin's journey to France, testifies to a work of "rewriting," or rather of *internal translation*, to which Hölderlin stubbornly dedicated his so-called "final years." The first version—and this should come as no surprise—is called "Dichtermut": "Poet's Courage," according to an old but still current sense of *Mut* in German. The second is called "Blödigkeit," a difficult word that is generally translated as "timidity," "diffidence," or "awkwardness."[13] But in both versions the motif of the poem is the same. It is the motif of the vocation or the mission of the poet, a vocation or mission that requires—let us use this word again—the archi-ethical quality of courage. Already we are on the very terrain where Heidegger will situate himself.

It is far from irrelevant, moreover, to point out that Benjamin's essay responds to what he too defines as a task: *eine Aufgabe*. This time, it is not the task of a teaching; but it is nonetheless the task of critique, or of what Benjamin calls, somewhat grandiloquently, the "aesthetics of the poetic art." And this task is governed by the search, in the poem, for what Benjamin refers to with the word that will be consistently used by Heidegger: *das Gedichtete*—a word that neither of them invents (it is found in Goethe) and which, as a concept, points for both of them toward the essence (or the Idea) of poetry. (The word is considered untranslatable because *dichten* is untranslatable. Following a suggestion of Beda Allemann, Maurice de Gandillac[14] bases his solution on the Latin *dictare* and proposes "*dictamen*," in a sense that he refers to as antiquated—though it is still understood in this sense by Rousseau, and many others after him—that is, as "the dictates of conscience." In an ethical sense, then. Faced with this difficulty, most of Heidegger's translators have chosen "the poetized."[15] This is perfectly acceptable, but the "hesitation" thus reveals all the more forcefully, if we can keep the two proposed solutions together, the link that unites the problematic of poetry to that of ethics.)

The question—the one dictated, if I can put it this way, by the task of criticism—is therefore the following: how to gain access to the *Gedichtete*—as *dictamen* or poetized? This is a question of method, a point continually underscored by Benjamin, who will never be concerned with demarcating himself from the vocabulary of philosophy, unlike Heidegger, who for his part will make such obstinate efforts to do so, particularly in opposition to the entirety of post-Cartesian metaphysics at least up to Hegel, by reducing *methodos* to *hodos: Weg, Wegmarken, Holzwege, unterwegs zu . . .,* etc. Despite several similarities in their "approaches," the problematic of access (which is a kind of breaking in) is not the problematic of wending one's way [*cheminement*]. The fact is that Benjamin does not speak in terms of essence, nor yet in terms of origin (though he will do so a little later). The language he uses here is a Kantian and post-Kantian language of the *a priori*. The major reference that supports his long "methodological" introduction is a fragment from Novalis: "Every work of art has in and of itself an *a priori* ideal, a necessity for being in the world."[16] If there is an aesthetics here (an "aesthetics of the poetic art"), this aesthetics is, in a somewhat unexpected sense, transcendental. The *dictamen,* which is above all not the cause of the poem or what would allow one to "explicate" it, and which in itself is nothing "poetic" (no more than is the essence of *Dichtung* in Heidegger), is purely and simply the condition of possibility of the poem. Its "precondition," as Benjamin says.

In order to establish this, Benjamin bases his demonstration on two concepts.

The first, borrowed from Goethe, is that of "inner form" (*innere Form*) or "content" (*Gehalt*)—a word to which, as we know, he will remain faithful throughout his critical enterprise, as attested for example by the essay written some five years later on Goethe's *Elective Affinities,* with its opposition between *Sachgehalt* [material content] and *Wahrheitsgehalt* [truth content].[17] This is how he introduces the concept, and we will see once again that here too it is, not by chance, a question of a task:

> The inner form, which Goethe characterized as content [*Gehalt*], shall be demonstrated in these poems. The poetic task, as the preliminary condition of an evaluation of the poem, is to be established. The evaluation cannot be guided by the way the poet has fulfilled his task; rather, the seriousness and greatness of the task itself determine the evaluation. For the task is derived from the poem itself. The task is also to be understood as the precondition of the poem, as the spiritual-intuitive [*geistig-anschaulich*] structure of the world to which the poem bears witness. This task, this precondition, shall be understood here as the ultimate basis accessible to analysis. Nothing will be said here about the

process of lyric composition, nothing about the person or world view of the creator; rather, the particular and unique sphere in which the task and precondition of the poem lie will be addressed.[18]

The precondition of the poem (its condition of possibility) is therefore the task, each time singular, of the poem—which is to say (and this amounts to the same) that to which the poem, in each case, bears witness. We will see in a moment that such a testimony is always a testimony of truth or, to the extent that it is singular and always singular, the attestation of *a* truth. And we must not forget that twenty years later Heidegger, too, will speak of testimony: In the Rome lecture based on the course—I will remain with this one example—he will stress that when Hölderlin speaks of language as "the most dangerous of all goods" (which therefore threatens truth itself), he defines it also as the gift that was given to man so that he might "testify to what he is."[19] It is of little importance here that Heidegger modifies the proposition and shifts from *what* man is to *who* he is, according to the politico-ontological aim I pointed out earlier. What is essential is that for him, as for Benjamin, whatever the differences in their interpretation of truth, poetry is defined as "saying the truth" or "speaking in the name of truth." If you like, poetry is the *martyr* of truth.[20] (This no doubt indicates why, from the moment when poetry is understood in this way, and by a sort of metonymic slippage, the poet's destiny effectively becomes that of a martyr. That is the case for the poets chosen by Heidegger, as it is for those who make up Alain Badiou's "pléiade." I will return to this point briefly below.)

Task, testimony: both of these, in their very unity (the task is testimony), thus constitute the precondition of the poem or its *a priori,* what one could call its authorization (an authorization that is very much prior to the authority of the poet, and prior twice over, since by authorizing the poem, it makes the poet). But in order for the complete definition of the *dictamen* to be fully accessible, a second concept is needed. This concept—we have already heard the word in passing—is the concept of "figure" (*Gestalt*), which brings with it, in an absolutely necessary fashion, the concept of "myth." This is how Benjamin introduces it—after refusing any examination of the creative process or the creative subject, he devotes his critique to the sole consideration of the "particular and unique sphere in which the task and precondition of the poem lie"; and he continues:

> This sphere is at once the product and the subject of this investigation. It itself can no longer be compared with the poem; it is, rather, the sole thing in this investigation that can be ascertained. This sphere, which for every poem has a special figure, is characterized as the *dictamen*. In this sphere that peculiar domain containing the truth of the poem shall be opened up. This "truth," which the most serious artists so insistently claim for their creations, shall be understood as the objectivity of their production, as the fulfillment of the artistic task in each case. [...] In its general character, the *dictamen* is the synthetic unity of two orders: intellect and intuition. This unity gains its particular figure as the inner form of the particular creation.[21]

The *dictamen* is therefore *Gestalt,* figure—a translation I maintain for the sake of economy. More precisely, the figure is for each poem the mode of presentation *and* of articulation of its inner form or of its content. But why is it a matter of a figure? Why this word—and this concept—*Gestalt*?

There are, it seems to me, two reasons for this.

The first is the one just given by Benjamin: In general, he says, the *dictamen* is a "synthetic unity of two orders," the order of the intellect (or spirit: *geistig*) and that of intuition. This vocabulary is obviously derived from Kant, following the model of the derivations carried out by Jena Romanticism ("spirit" for "understanding," for example). If I am not mistaken, then, this proposition amounts quite simply to saying that the *dictamen* is the *transcendental schema* of the poem. *Dichten,* "poetizing," is referred to the transcendental imagination, that "art concealed in the depths of the human soul."[22] Or, to invoke a category that I like to use in recalling the breakthrough attempted by Heidegger between the *Kantbuch* and the lectures on the "Origin of the Work of Art," it is referred to an originary *technē*, which founds a world because it is an archaic or principial configuration (*Gestaltung*) of the world. In Benjamin's language: the *dictamen* is a "limit-concept," a limit between the poem itself and that to which it bears witness, that to which it attests in its truth—which Benjamin calls "life"—since it is the condition of one *as well as* the other. It ensures the "transition" between two "functional unities," that of the poem (prior to the distinction between form and matter) and that of life (prior to the distinction between task and solution). But the simplest way to continue here is to quote:

> Through this relation to the intuitive and spiritual functional unity of the poem, the *dictamen* emerges as a limit-determination with respect to the poem. At the same time, however, it is a limit-concept with respect to another functional unity, since a limit-concept is possible only as a limit between two concepts. This other functional unity, now, is the idea of the task, corresponding to the idea of the solution as which the poem exists. (For task and solution can be separated only in the abstract.) For the creator, this idea of task is always life. In it lies the other extreme functional unity. Thus, the *dictamen* emerges as the transition from the functional unity of life to that of the poem. In the *dictamen,* life determines itself through the poem, the task through the solution. The underlying basis is not the individual life-mood of the artist but rather a life-context determined by art.[23]

Again, if I understand correctly, the *dictamen,* as *Gestalt,* is a figure of existence. Or, in other words, life (existence)—inasmuch as the task of the poem is to bear witness to it—is itself, in its truth, poetic. A poem can say, in truth, that we live (exist) in truth. That is, poetically. ("Full of merit, but poetically, man dwells on this earth," reads a line from Hölderlin on which, some years later, Heidegger will comment at length.[24]) Poetry is our destiny. A *dictamen,* in fact.

Hence, I believe, the second reason that Benjamin provides to justify the word—the concept—*Gestalt* (a word—a concept—that is very "charged" during the period when he uses it, both from a philosophical [less Hegelian than Nietzschean] and political point of view: It will be one of the key words of the "conservative revolution" that is beginning to emerge). Benjamin remains very prudent. He is speaking, he says, "approximately." Nonetheless: *Gestalt* refers to myth; or, if you prefer: every figure (but one could also say: every model, or every example) is potentially mythic, not in a sense that is abstract or distant from myth, but in the sense in which life itself (existence) is—to borrow Thomas Mann's formula from 1936—"life in the myth": that is, "citation."[25] Here is what Benjamin says: "The categories in which this sphere, the transitional sphere of the two functional unities, can be grasped do not yet have adequate models and should perhaps more readily be associated with the concepts of myth. It is precisely the feeblest artistic achievements that refer to the immediate feeling of life; whereas the strongest, with respect to their truth, refer to a sphere related to the mythic: the *dictamen*. One could say that life is, in general, the *dictamen* of poems [*das Gedichtete der Gedichte*]."[26]

The mythic thus understood is above all not the mythological, that is, the stereotyped organization (or cohesion) of mythemes, the weakening of their reciprocal relations. The mythic—which *is* the *dictamen,* or which the *dictamen is*—is existence itself in its *configuration* or in its *figurability.* That is why the poem is at bottom a gesture of existence—in view of existence. The poem, to remain with Benjamin's vocabulary, is a figure of life. Which amounts to saying that life is poetic. Essentially. Not because it is "poetizable" (that would be the mystification par excellence: mythology), but because the *dictamen* of poems—which is never this or that particular poem from which, however, it is indissociable—dictates life.

Here the *dictamen* is *courage.* This is perhaps the *dictamen* of all dictation, the poetized of every poem. Or of literature in general. Benjamin, in any case, considered the possibility:

> The law according to which all apparent elements of sensation and ideas come to light as the embodiments of essential, in principle infinite functions is called the Law of Identity. This term describes the synthetic unity of functions. It may be recognized in each particular figure it takes as an *a priori* of the poem. [...] Until the applicability of this method to the aesthetics of the lyric as such and perhaps to other domains has been tested, further exposition is not in order. Only then can one clearly perceive the *a priori* of the individual poem, that of the poem in general, or even that of other literary genres or of literature in general.[27]

The *dictamen* is therefore—let us remain for the moment with this prudent localization—courage: "The Poet's Courage."

It is not my intention to reconstruct Benjamin's demonstration. I will give no more than its principle—and, moreover, in a rather dry manner, for which I apologize in advance. This principle is relatively simple, whereas the demonstration, for its part, is very complex.

"The Poet's Courage" is from the beginning, as Benjamin remarks, a mythological *topos.* And it is treated as such by Hölderlin in the first version of the poem. It is the *topos* of the properly heroic poet, the intercessor or mediator between the gods and men (other more or less contemporaneous poems speak of the poet as a demigod, and this is precisely the motif on which Heidegger will focus his attention) and consequently braving the greatest risks in order to fulfill his task or his mission. Benjamin's judgment, since criticism is a matter of judgment, is that the simple repetition of the topos alone explains the poem's weakness: Neither does the relation of the human to the divine (or of the poet to the god whom he invokes as his model) escape convention, nor is the essence of the divine (that is to say, its inscription of death within existence) truly grasped. The poem is powerless to give figure to a world:

> In the first version of his poem, Hölderlin's subject is a destiny—the death of the poet. Hölderlin praises in song the sources of the courage to die this death. This death is the center from which the world of poetic dying was meant to arise. Existence in that world would be the poet's courage. But here only the most vigilant intuition can have a glimmer of this structure of laws from a world of the poet. The voice rises up timidly at first to sing a cosmos, whose own decline is signified by the death of the poet. But the myth is developed from mythology. The sun god is the poet's ancestor, and his death is the destiny through which the poet's death, at first mirrored, becomes real. [. . .] The poem lives in the Greek world; a beauty modeled on that of Greece animates it, and it is dominated by the mythology of the Greeks. The particular principle of Greek creation, however, is not fully manifest. "For, ever since the poem escaped from mortal lips / Breathing peace, benefiting in sorrow and happiness / Our song brought joy to the hearts / Of men." These words give only a feeble hint of the awe that filled Pindar—and also the late Hölderlin—before the figure of the poetic. Neither do the "bards of the people," "pleasing to all," thus seen, serve to give this poem an intuitive world foundation. The figure of the dying sun god testifies most clearly to an unmastered duality in all its elements. Idyllic nature still plays its special role opposite the figure of the god. Beauty, in other words, has not yet wholly become form.[28]

In the second version, however, the mythologeme of the setting sun, of decline, of twilight, etc., is abandoned. And with it that of the mediating hero and the bards of the people. Benjamin's intuition here is that by ridding itself of the mythological, the second version paradoxically reinforces the mythic by which it seeks, as we know, to think the *dictamen*. The *dictamen* appears in its truth—or the essence of courage is attained—only after the mythological has collapsed: at the precise point of its failure. Benjamin speaks of the "deposition of the mythological."[29] Later, still in relation to Hölderlin and against Heidegger's interpretation, Adorno will speak of "demythologization."[30] Such a failure of the mythological is quite obviously accompanied by a certain failure of the theological. In any case by a certain theologico-political dissociation. I will return to this.

The deposition of the mythological is a deliberate gesture: it moves in the direction of objectivity and the concrete, which is to say that, technically speaking (if you will), it moves toward a sort of literalization, a prosaism, a phrasing removed from the register of eloquence and classical pathos. And toward the abandonment of the stereotypes of sacralization. I will give one example, that of the reworking of the first two lines—on which, as it happens, Benjamin insists very little. The first version says:

> Are not all the living related to you?
> Does not the Parca herself nourish you for her service?

This is indeed the traditional *topos* of death: the Parca, absolute servitude before death, the community of all mortals (the "living"). In the second version, however, we read, in a rhythm that remains the same:

> Are not many of the living known to you?
> Does not your foot stride upon what is true, as upon
>   carpets?

"Many of the living" replaces "all the living," "known" replaces "related": This is a first step toward objectivization, a first renunciation of the abstraction of "the mortals," a first determination of "the living" (those who are "known"). This immediately brings with it, in the second line, both an abandonment of the nominal reference to the Parca and the literalization of the mythologeme: from the threads of the "many" destinies is woven something like the carpet of death or rather of the dead, that is, the carpet woven by mortal destinies, the very one we ceaselessly step on, which is the truth of mortal being. Or death, not in its truth, but as truth. And it is because the second version attains this truth that the *dictamen* of courage can suddenly appear in all its force. At the end of his demonstration, Benjamin has no difficulty in stating this new determination of courage—the most just and correct there is, provided that we agree to read Hölderlin through to the end:

> The *dictamen* of the first version initially knows courage only as a quality. Man and death stand rigid, opposing each other; they share no intuitable world. To be sure, the attempt was already made to find a deep relation to death in the poet, in his divine-natural existence, yet only indirectly through the mediation of the god, to whom death in a mythological sense belonged and to whom the poet, once again in a mythological sense, was approximated. [. . .] Thus the duality of man and death could be based only on a lax feeling of life. It ceased to exist, since the *dictamen* marshaled its forces into a deeper coherence, and a spiritual principle—courage—fashioned life from itself. Courage is self-abandon to the danger that threatens the world. It conceals a peculiar paradox, which for the first time permits the structure of the *dictamen* of both versions to be fully understood: The danger exists for the courageous person, yet he does not heed it. For he would be a coward if he heeded it; and if it did not exist for him, he would not be courageous. This strange relation dissolves, in that the danger threatens not the courageous one himself but rather the world. Courage is the life-feeling of the man who surrenders himself to danger, so that in his death he expands that danger into a danger for the world and at the same time overcomes it.

And, a little later, "The world of the dead hero is a new mythical one, steeped in danger; this is the world of the second version of the poem. In it a spiritual principle has become completely dominant: The heroic poet becomes one with the world. The poet does not have to fear death; he is a hero because he lives the center of all relations. The principle of the *dictamen* as such is the supreme sovereignty of relation."[31] Spiritual principle (the word *spiritual* occurs twice), sovereignty of relation: The *dictamen* of courage attests to the congruence—or the "fittingness": "Yet we ourselves / Bring fitting [*Schickliche*] hands," we read at the end of the second version—between (poetic) heroism and the danger of the world. And that is indeed the point where the mythological fails, or even the theological, if both consist in the separation of "elements" and the refusal of "relation." Commenting finally on the third stanza of the last version, in order to point out the "sublation of the order of mortals and heavenly ones," Benjamin indicates forcefully, "One can assume that the words 'a lonely deer' characterize men; and this fits in very well with the title of this poem. 'Timidity' has now become the authentic stance of the poet. Since he has been transposed into the middle of life, nothing awaits him but motionless existence, complete passivity, which is the essence of the courageous man—nothing except to surrender himself wholly to relation."[32]

Failure of the mythological (of the theological): I believe that we can speak even more precisely of "deconstruction," in the very sense that Heidegger began to give this term, although—unlike Benjamin, who however does not use this concept—he does not see to what extent it is at work in Hölderlin's last poems. That is, to what extent it *unworks* them. In a very clear and decisive manner, Benjamin finds the basis of this "deconstruction" in the principle of *sobriety* as it is set forth by Hölderlin in his "Remarks" on the translations of Sophocles, as the guiding principle of modern poetry. Or, if you like, as that which dictates to poetry its proper task. At the end of his essay, Benjamin writes the following; its political, and more than political, significance should be immediately apparent:

> In the course of this investigation, the word "sobriety" was deliberately avoided, a word that might often have served for purposes of characterization. Only now shall Hölderlin's phrase "sacredly sober" be uttered, now that its understanding has been determined. Others have noted that these words exhibit the tendency of his later creations. They arise from the inner certainty with which those works stand in his own spiritual life, in which sobriety now is allowed, is demanded, because this life is in itself sacred, standing—beyond all elevation—in the sublime. Is this life still that of Hellenism? That is as little the case here as it is that a pure work of art could ever be that of a people; and as little the case, too, that it could be that of an individual, or anything other than this proper element which we find in the *dictamen*.[33]

And so that matters will be quite clear, I will quote the following, which is the very end of the essay. "The contemplation of the *dictamen*, however, leads not to myth but rather—in the greatest creations—only to mythic connections, which in the work of art are shaped into unique, unmythological, and unmythic forms that cannot be better understood by us.

"But if there were words with which to grasp the relation between myth and the inner life from which the later poem sprang, it would be those of Hölderlin from a period still later than that of this poem: 'Myths, which take leave of the earth, / ... They return to mankind.'"[34]

In other words, there is no way to attach any theologico-politics to this *failing* theologico-poetics. No historial mission of the Poem or the Hymn. Sobriety, as we know, is what Benjamin, a few years later in his thesis on Jena Romanticism, will identify with prose, using the speculative terms borrowed in this case from Fichte: "The Idea of poetry is prose."[35] And for this very reason he will make Hölderlin the secret—eccentric—center of Romanticism. We could thus risk saying, in a lapidary fashion: Sobriety is the courage of poetry. Or, The courage of poetry is prose. Which of course does not exclude versification.

Courage of poetry: The phrase can be heard or stressed in two different ways.

On the one hand, it is a question of a subjective genitive: Courage here is poetry's courage for itself, poetry's courage for poetry (we could call this its stubbornness), and in the discovery of the poetized or the *dictamen*, we are dealing with something like an archi-ethics of poetizing as such: the poem is the archi-ethical act. We are in the order of what the Romantics called "reflection," or even, up to a certain point, in the (Heideggerian) order of "the poetry of poetry." The regime is one of pure intransitivity. In Benjamin's reading, courage of poetry means courage to leave behind the mythological, to break with it and to deconstruct it. It is the courage to invent poetry, to configure the Poem as the testimony that it is. Thus the destiny of poetry, after what Jean-Christophe Bailly calls "the end of the Hymn," would indeed be prose as the poem's "speaking-the-true" about the Poem.

On the other hand, it is a matter of an objective genitive: Courage is the courage that poetry must have in its transitive (prophetic or angelic) function, by which it would confront a danger to the world and would announce a task to fulfill. The ethical act would then be less the Poem itself than what the Poem dictates as a task. And perhaps we would no longer be in the order of the archi-ethical, if the archi-ethical, unlike ethics, is an ethics that does not know what the good is. (I propose this distinction in the wake of Lacan's discourse in Seminar 7, *The Ethics of Psychoanalysis*;[36] but also indeed in the wake of Heidegger's discourse in the "Letter on 'Humanism.'") Or if the archi-ethical, as we might put it, has the obligation—perhaps impossible to keep, but that is its immeasurable responsibility—to tear itself away from the (mimetic) ethics of the example, the most ancient and the most ruinous that we know of. It involves the cult of heroes and the metonymic slippage from the martyrdom of poetry (as testimony) to the becoming-martyr of the poet. You recall that (1) Hölderlin is the poet of poets and the poet of poetry. [. . .] (3) Hölderlin is the poet of poets insofar as he is the poet of the Germans. From one proposition to the other, the "poet of poetry" has been forgotten. An entire politics is thus decided.

We must not be too quick to believe that this difference of inflection or of emphasis is what constitutes the dividing line between Benjamin and Heidegger, even if in the ideological or political register (which is to say also in the philosophical register) things—as of now—are perfectly clear and the difference could not be more decisive. In reality, for both Benjamin and Heidegger—but certainly not in the same way—intransitivity and transitivity do not cease to encroach upon one another. And it is a matter, in both cases, of what poetry testifies to in attesting to itself as such, that is, in attesting to itself in its relation to truth, in its *saying the truth*. Is it a (modern) vocation to martyrdom? Courage itself? Yes, but in the mode of failure. And yes, on the condition of admitting finally that what is testified to is the "default of God [*Gottes Fehl*]," as Hölderlin said, or—what amounts to the same thing—of our *a-theist* condition.

May this be understood as a tribute and salutation to Benjamin. The humblest and most grateful possible.

Postscript

There is no discussion after the *Conférences du Perroquet:* That is the rule, and it is an excellent one. But nothing prevents conversations from taking place afterward, as was the case on the evening of June 23, 1993, between Alain Badiou and myself. This exchange came after a dialogue, initiated several years before, on what Badiou calls "the age of the poets" (a reference is made to this in the lecture). A few days later, in a letter, Alain Badiou formulated the principle of his objection—which in fact is not really an objection. I would like to cite the essential moment of his argument:

> If it turns out that the immanent operation of the poem, already—or even especially—for Hölderlin, is in no way the establishment of the sovereignty of myth (or of sacred names), but on the contrary their erasure, and therefore a becoming prose; *then* the mytheme is not an intrinsic given properly located in the poem, but, already, a speculative appropriation that does violence to the poem. In that case, are you not calling "mytheme" the very thing that I am calling "suture"? For I have always conceived the suture as an operation carried out *by philosophy,* in some way grafted onto certain aspects that have been unilaterally detached and isolated from the post-Romantic poem. And I would agree [. . .] that the ultimate destination of this operation is theo-logico-political.
>
> In the final analysis, it is a matter, for both of us (tell me if I am mistaken), of *thinking the 1930s.* With regard to this undertaking (at the heart of which is an attempt to think Nazism as a politics), are not "suture" and "mytheme" notions whose origins are certainly singular (and very different in each case), but whose convergence is possible, or even probable?

I have only one word to add to this statement—but it will be understood why I would like to add it here: The convergence is not only possible or probable, it is, it seems to me, quite real.

Epilogue: The Spirit of National
Socialism and Its Destiny

The hypothesis from which I begin is that National Socialism is in
no way an aberrant or incomprehensible phenomenon but rather is
inscribed in a perfectly rigorous manner in the so-called "spiritual"
history of Germany. Only a historico-philosophical interpretation is
capable of providing access to National Socialism in its essence, that
is, to what gives it its singularity in comparison to analogous phenomena in the first half of the twentieth century (which for the sake
of convenience we can call "totalitarianisms") and to what makes it
an exception.

This hypothesis is authorized, in turn, by an explication of Heidegger's political thought. And by an explicit confrontation *with* it. Heidegger is not considered here as a Nazi thinker (which, however, he *also*
was, albeit briefly), but as the thinker of National Socialism, which he
both acknowledged and concealed.

The proposition "Heidegger is the thinker of National Socialism"
means that Heidegger attempted to think—and he is probably the only
one to do so—the *unthought* of National Socialism, what he himself
called in 1935 "the inner truth and greatness of the Movement."[1] But
nothing here is self-evident: first because the difficulty was—and remains—immense (and it is indeed necessary to see that the unthought
of National Socialism perhaps remained the unthought of Heidegger
himself); also because uncovering, or attempting to uncover, the unthought of National Socialism supposed that any merely political, historical, or philosophical interpretation of the phenomenon be rejected
in advance. In other words, Heidegger's political preaching is entirely
encrypted: It is not a political preaching, and, in order to hear it, it is
necessary to take a step beyond—or rather back from—the political,

a step that this preaching calls for in the direction of its essence which, for its part, is nothing political. Such a step, which is that of thought itself, is riskier than the one required by the fundamental ontology of *Being and Time*, a project that was in fact abandoned in 1934–35, when it became a question of preparing the "withdrawal"—in fact quite relative (except in his teaching)—from National Socialism.

The logic of withdrawal is abyssal, as we know: Every withdrawal traces and draws out that from which it withdraws.[2] Political disavowal is the touchstone of fascism. It is certainly at work in Heidegger's discourse in the 1930s and beyond—even up to the end. Nevertheless, this disavowal must not be confused with any sort of a-politicism or anti-politicism, which was in fact commonplace in the average ideology of the "conservative revolution" since at least 1918 (or even, in its "anti" form, in the far Left discourse on democracy). The disavowal of the political in Heidegger is made in the name of the essence or the origin of the political, of what I propose to call the archi-political. After the defeat in 1945, Heidegger—in what was almost his first public gesture—denounced ethics (humanism) in the name of an archi-ethics, that is, in the name of an originary understanding of *ēthos*;[3] likewise, in response to National Socialism—which obviously implies a responsibility—he sought to think an archi-politics: *polis*, he says in 1935, does not refer to any "politics," a word he always uses in quotation marks; *polis* signifies the *Da* of *Sein* (the *there* of *being*).[4] One year later he included the institution of a *polis*, a state, among the inaugural modes of instituting or positing truth (*alētheia*), placing it alongside the work of art, the proximity of the supreme being, authentic sacrifice (which, as Kantorowicz said, was probably "sacrifice for the fatherland"),[5] and the questioning of thought.[6]

That is the reason, if it is after all necessary to define Heidegger's "political" position, why I believe I am justified in speaking of an *archi-fascism* (which, despite some troubling proximities, is quite different from the "sur-fascism" of which Breton did not hesitate to accuse Bataille during the same period).

Under these conditions, what does Heidegger's archi-fascism invite us to think concerning the unthought of National Socialism?

(Let me point out beforehand that the propositions I will present are extremely schematic; in reality they are based on long and detailed analyses that I cannot present here. I apologize for this in advance.)

1. National Socialism is the fulfillment of the Western history of *technē*—or rather: of Western history *as* the history of *technē*.

One of the basic commonplaces of European reactionary thought after World War I is that the modern age is determined as the age of technics, whether one deplores it or makes a call to take up the challenge it poses. It is not by chance that for more than twenty years Heidegger remained very attached to the two books by Ernst Jünger that so marked the age: *Die Totale Mobilmachung* (Total Mobilization) and *Der Arbeiter* (The Worker); or that after the fact, at the very beginning of the 1950s, he could still specify what he meant in 1935 by "the inner truth and greatness of the Movement" (which he amends to "of this movement") by speaking of the "encounter between global technics and modern man."[7] From the point of view of the most radical fascism, the Marxist ontology of work and production (or of the auto-production of man) represents only a first stammering of the coming thought of the new age. Technics is the truth of Work.

Aside from the fact that he never subscribed for a moment to the "Nietzscheanism" fabricated by the intellectuals and ideologues of the so-called "Movement" (from 1935 to 1941, he even devoted most of his teaching to a deconstruction of Nietzsche's metaphysics), what nonetheless distinguishes Heidegger is the "step backward" that he attempts to take in the interpretation of *technē:* he not only goes back from science to knowledge (*das Wissen*), which is invariably the word he uses to translate the Greek *technē* (after all, this gesture was already constitutive of speculative Idealism); but under the more commonly admitted sense of "art," he also aims at an *archi-technē*, which obliges him to deconstruct the entirety of "Western aesthetics," from Plato and Aristotle to Hegel and Nietzsche. ("The Will to Power as Art," a course given in 1936, is explicit in this regard.) The "withdrawal" of 1934–35 leads to the "Origin of the Work of Art" and produces, consequently, the truth of National Socialism as what I call national-aestheticism.[8] Which suffices to indicate its "insufficiency."

2. National-aestheticism (my reading of Heidegger forces this some-

what monstrous formulation on me) is a difficult notion to handle. To use an expedient that Heidegger himself used—concerning the relation between *Gestell* (the essence of technics) and *Ereignis* (being as its own proper advent)—we could say that national-aestheticism is to Heidegger's thought of art and the "political" (or the historial) what a more or less well-developed photograph is to its negative. But even this indication in the direction of negativity is excessive here. It is in any case because National Socialism is imprisoned not by a particular aesthetics, but by aesthetics itself—as the aesthetic apprehension of art—that it is merely National Socialism. Or, if you will, and in order to abbreviate: It is because it allowed the Wagnerian din to drown out and conceal the voice of Hölderlin.

3. Excluding the so-to-speak unique reference to Hölderlin, Heidegger's poietico-political program is virtually indistinguishable from the Romantic program, if we recognize, as Benjamin did, that Romanticism was the last modern—and therefore revolutionary—movement that sought to "save the tradition." The "conservative revolution" was precisely that. (We must not forget that the only publication on which Heidegger collaborated during the regime was the more or less oppositional journal—in any case only two issues were printed—edited by Ernesto Grassi, Walter Otto, and Karl Reinhardt, *Geistige Überlieferung* [Spiritual Tradition].) There are even some stubborn adherences to Romanticism, by way of Nietzsche, particularly the "Untimely Meditation" on history, from which it will take Heidegger a very long time to detach himself (which does not happen until the lecture on technology and, especially, the letter to Jünger from 1955, "Zur Seinsfrage").[9]

Among these adherences, the most primary and resistant is the one formed by the notion of *Gestalt*, borrowed more from Nietzsche than from Hegel. This notion allows him to think the essence of the work of art—certainly in a complex manner, since the vocabulary of incision, the trait and the trace (*reissen*, *Riss*, etc.) never ceases to interfere—beyond or on this side of *Bilden* and the image (*Bild* [image], *Bildung* [formation], *bildende Kraft* [formative power] or *Einbildungskraft* [imagination]). It is in relation to the work of art that in 1936 Heidegger risks for the first time the word *Gestell* (enframing) to designate the unity of all the modes of *stellen* and *stehen*, that is, of the *thesis* of truth. This motif is extremely important because it brings with it the preformal or "pre-eidetic" values of the plastic or of fiction/figuration (*plassein, fingere*), of fashioning, of the stroke (*Schlag*)—Nietzsche's "philosophizing with a hammer"—and of *Geschlecht*, the imprint or the impression—or, to speak Greek, of the *type*. (But with regard to *Geschlecht*, I refer to Jacques Derrida's reading of Heidegger's reading of Trakl;[10] the word also means genus or species, race, family or descent, lineage, sex, and gender—the semantic drift is abyssal.) It is for this reason that I have proposed to define Heidegger's archi-fascist ontology, by shifting and altering one of its own formulas, as an onto-typo-logy—the very one that he ended up demarcating or delimiting in Jünger, and consequently in Nietzsche, although he did not consent to recognize that it was in effect the "truth" of "biologism" and "racial hygiene," and the justification, in the final instance, of the program of Extermination.[11]

The fascist obsession is in fact the obsession with figuration, *Gestaltung*. It is a matter both of erecting a figure (engaging in the properly monumental work of a sculptor, as Nietzsche thought) and of producing, according to this model, not a type of man but *the* type of humanity—or an absolutely typical humanity. From a philosophical point of view, it is ultimately a question of overturning the Platonic critique of archaic—heroic and aristocratic—pedagogy, founded on the imitation (the *mimēsis*) of examples, as it initiates the political project of the *Republic*. In the sections of *Being and Time* on History, Heidegger writes that it is by choosing its "heroes" in the tradition—which involves a decision—that *Dasein* can open its historial possibilities.[12] In 1933, in the Rectoral Address, the hero thus chosen is Nietzsche, the prophet of the death of God.[13] Some months later, as a sign of "withdrawal" and of an explicit entry into a "political" discourse—albeit in a sense so lofty that he has no need to "talk about the political"—the hero is Hölderlin, the poet mediator or the demi-god, who is the poet of poetry (that is, precisely of the essence of art) only because he is—or ought to be—the "poet of the Germans."[14] (That the Germans are said still to be "indebted" in relation to Hölderlin, and therefore not yet to have come to themselves as such, suffices then to indicate the *insufficiency*—a term I want to stress—of National Socialism.)

4. In a register that is hardly distinct from the previous one, this obsession with the figure is an obsession with myth. In the (abject) world of desacralization and "disenchantment" (of *Entzauberung* in Max Weber's sense, which is in fact not far removed from the impulses behind the "conservative revolution," as Domenico Losurdo has clearly shown;[15] but Heidegger spoke more radically of *Entgötterung,* the de-divinization or the becoming a-theist of the world), the watchword, since early Romanticism and the "Oldest System-Program of German Idealism," is that of a "new mythology." Wagner's *Ring* and Nietzsche's *Zarathustra* did little more than complete the program. This means that, once the time was past for the *imitatio Christi* or the *imitatio sanctorum* as the source of theologico-political authority or Catholic (universal) Christianity, after the discrediting of the secular civil Republic—which was always only half secular, from supreme Being to consecrated emperors—and after the exposure of the Enlightenment's failure, especially after World Catastrophe I, an appeal was made to myth (which could also be, as in Georges Sorel, the myth of the general strike) as the only chance for restoring meaning and giving order to our being-in-common.

Once again, I will speak very schematically: It is indeed necessary to see that the collapse of catholicity produced the modern political as a contradiction—between the promise of a universality (the rights of man) and the refoundation of national communities in the form of nation-states (the rights of the citizen). The imperialist exportation of the French Revolution inaugurated the age of national wars, the age of wars between peoples, that was announced by Fichte; and these wars were all the more powerful in that they eventually became associated with the war between philosophical doctrines as evoked by Nietzsche (Nietzscheanism versus Marxism). Everywhere in the twentieth century, the new man will be that of a people, or even a race; and "eternal Russia" (whether "caesarist" or Czarist) will have quickly done away with proletarian internationalism—except in its police version, of course (the *Komintern*).

Myth—*die Sage,* in Heidegger's vocabulary—re-emerged in this way only because it was thought to be originarily linked to the being-of-a-people: to "peoplehood." Myth is the originary Poem (*Urgedicht*) of every people. For all Romantic politics, this means that a people originates, exists as such, or identifies and appropriates itself—that is, it is properly itself—only on the basis of myth. When Herder, Hegel, or Heidegger repeats Herodotus's statement that "it is Homer who gave to Greece its gods," they mean nothing other than that. According to the mimetic logic or the mimetologic evoked a moment ago, myth is the means of identification (this idea is still powerful, however complex its re-elaboration, all the way up to Freud's last works, as well as Thomas Mann's); and the appeal to myth is a demand for the *appropriation of the means of identification,* judged in the end to be more decisive than that of the "means of production."

5. Heidegger's thought, on this point as on others, is at least subtler and more slippery than this generalized Romanticism. He leaves to the "thinkers" of the Party (Bertram, Krieck, and Bäumler) the concern with a naïve opposition between *Mythos* and *Logos,* and to Rosenberg the task of defining, in response to nihilism and the Spenglerian decline, "the myth of the twentieth century." But an analogous logic underpins both his radicalization of the concept of nihilism (extended to metaphysics as a whole) and his determination of the essence of art (as *Dichtung, Sprache,* and *Sage,* in that order, as we know). As well as, consequently, his appeal to Hölderlin.

Heidegger thereby enables us not only to understand the political stakes of art in the modern age; he also makes it possible to understand that art, *technē*—that is, for him, *archi-technē*—is what is at stake in the modern political. He says the truth of Goebbels's response to Furt-wängler, which was merely a somnambulistic repetition of Napoleon and Nietzsche: that the true artist, the one who fashions in the highest sense, is the statesman. Or, in a register that is after all closer to his own, Heidegger says the truth of Hegel's tripartite determination of the Greek work of art: as the "athletic body" (the subjective moment; the formula, which comes from Winckelmann, is also found in Hölderlin), as the pantheon named in language or fashioned in marble (objective moment), and as the City (subjective-objective moment).

But what he says in this way is, in reality, the truth of the German destiny.

6. The modern political, in the very difficulty it has of instituting

itself, does not begin with the French Revolution but, as Heine and Marx suspected, with the Reform (the radicalization of Christianity, that is, of a-theism) and the Renaissance (the imitation of the Ancients). In both cases, although in a different manner, it is Rome that is shaken up—both as Empire and as Church. But if the nations of the properly Roman regions remain caught in Latinity (the French Revolution repeats the republican *gestus,* and the return to antiquity in Italy as in France is filtered through the Hellenistic and Roman imitation of the Greeks), if in these nations the dislocation of the theologico-political leaves the Catholic religion relatively vital, it is quite otherwise with the peoples—more or less lumped together—formerly situated beyond the *limes,* which is and remains the frontier of Lutheranism: the peoples of Tacitus's *Germania* and of Kleist's *Hermannsschlacht* or *Battle of Arminius.* These are the "poorly converted" of whom Freud spoke. These peoples—although Hegel baptized the entire Christian age since the fall of Rome as the "Germanic world," and despite the existence of the Germanic Holy Roman Empire—never belonged to World History (*Weltgeschichte*) as politically identifiable peoples, that is, as properly national peoples. What the *spiritual* history of Germany indicates—and there is one, it is even *the* history of Germany—is that Germany (the homeland of poets and thinkers, as Heidegger said, or of the "metaphysical people par excellence," in the formula of Mme. de Staël) is lacking in identity [*en défaut d'identité*]. "German distress," *die deutsche Not,* has but one meaning: *Germany does not exist.* This fundamentally determines the elegiac essence of German art, or its melancholy genius. (Thomas Mann, at the time of *Doctor Faustus,* wrote some decisive pages on this subject.)

Modern political identification assumes and engages a harsh agonistic, in the sense of this word that Nietzsche took from the Greeks. In the appropriation of the means of identification, it is a matter of "mimetic rivalry" and its formidable double bind: "We must imitate the Ancients," said Winckelmann, "in order to make ourselves inimitable in turn." This was to state at the very least that the German agonistic had to demarcate itself from the Latin type of *imitatio,* that is, from the cultural imperialism of Italy or France—from Rome. As Bäumler wrote in 1931 (in *Nietzsche, der Philosoph und Politiker*), though he was far from being the only one to use this language: "Germany can exist in universal history only as Greater Germany. She has no choice but to be either the anti-Roman power of Europe, or not to be. [...] Only nordic Germany could be the creator of a Europe that will be more than a Roman colony, the Germany of Hölderlin and Nietzsche."[16] From this point of view, Germany was in effect the site of a radicalized *Kulturkampf* in which, as we know, it was an altogether different antiquity from the one transmitted by the tradition—an altogether different Greece—that sought to invent itself as the origin and the model of an incomparable destination.

That is what was transmitted by the Nietzscheanism that unfolded throughout the course of the century, and it is what, in the historical turmoil, led to the establishment of the Nazi political as a "total artwork"—and not merely to fascism as the "aestheticization of politics," in which case we probably would not have gone beyond Italian opera....

7. In Heidegger, this agonistic governs three fundamental motifs. To conclude, I will limit myself to enumerating them. An examination of them would take us farther than we can go here today.

a. The motif of *Heimatlosigkeit* (or of "uprootedness" [*déracinement*], to transcribe the term into the vocabulary of the far Right in France, from Barrès to Maurras and beyond). It is a question, says Heidegger in 1946, of the fundamental historial experience of Europe, which Nietzsche, imprisoned as he was in the nihilism he denounced, failed to experience all the way to the end and which Marx alone—besides Hölderlin, of course—was able to think by placing the age under the sign of alienation: *Ent-fremdung*, becoming foreign or strange.

From this perspective, one could show that the various fascisms, as well as Marxism in its Russian interpretation, are merely a response to the generalized homelessness or "uncanniness" [*dépaysement*][17] of the modern age, to the mass dislocation of a centuries-old peasantry, organized within hardly a century by industry and Capital. Heidegger knows this more than he wants not to know it.

b. The motif of *Wiederholung*, the repetition of the greatness of the (Greek) inception of the Western destiny insofar as this greatness never properly took place (and that is the logic of the unthought), and insofar as it forms, on that very basis, the future or the "to-come" [*l'à-venir*] of "our" History. This motif comes in fact from the second of Nietzsche's *Untimely Meditations,* but it is also found in Paul de Lagarde: "For while you turn your eyes and your heart toward new things, with every breath I live in a past that never was and that is the only future to which I aspire" (quoted by Botho Strauss in *Anschwellender Bocksgesang*);[18] or among the faithful in Stefan George's "Circle," such as Hugo von Hofmannsthal, who construes authentic history as the narration of "what did not take place" (a formula that Benjamin could have countersigned). That said, it remains true that Heidegger takes a step back from *imitatio,* a step meant to point up the weakness, not to say the kitsch, of mass art and of the imperial monumentality of the totalitarianisms. Heidegger's examples of the Greek temple or Van Gogh's shoes, from the 1936 lectures on art, have been the target of much irony (and many attempts at glossing over). One would do better to situate these examples in relation to the unforgiving critique of the Wagnerian project.

c. The theologico-political motif: What Heidegger is seeking in the Hölderlinian preaching—in the *Sage,* in myth, which, as he will say, is not the *Heldensaga*—is the promise of a new god: "Nur ein Gott kann uns noch retten." Only a god can save us now. This, we recall, is Heidegger's testamentary statement, his last word.

The lamentation over an "existential" loss, the appeal to a recommencement, the listening to the poem as "gospel": all this constitutes or configures—very near, and very far from, messianic utopianism—the hope of a religion. Through which we might perceive, at the bedrock of the "totalitarianisms," the restoration—profane only with regard to Christianity—of political religion. Or, if you prefer: of religion *tout court.* But that is another matter. . . . And we will not find our way out of it without further examination.

Notes

Unless otherwise indicated, (1) all notes are the translator's; the author's notes, with the exception of some bibliographical references, are marked as such; (2) all interpolations of foreign languages in quotations (other than French) are the author's. English translations will be cited with modifications as necessary.

Translator's Introduction: The Courage of Thought

1. Martin Heidegger, "Das Ende der Philosophie und die Aufgabe des Denkens," in *Zur Sache des Denkens,* 3d ed. (Tübingen: Max Niemeyer, 1988), 61–80. English translation: "The End of Philosophy and the Task of Thinking," in *On Time and Being,* trans. Joan Stambaugh (New York: Harper and Row, 1972), 55–73.

2. Heidegger's postwar writings on Hölderlin consist of no more than a handful of lectures, including most notably ". . . dichterisch wohnet der Mensch . . ." (1951) published in Heidegger, *Vorträge und Aufsätze* (Pfullingen: Neske, 1954), 181–98; hereafter, "Dichterisch." English translation: ". . . Poetically Man Dwells . . .," in *Poetry, Language, Thought,* trans. Albert Hofstadter (New York: Harper and Row, 1971), 213–29; hereafter, "Poetically."

3. Heidegger, *Erläuterungen zu Hölderlins Dichtung,* 6th ed. (Frankfurt am Main: Klostermann, 1996), 29–30; hereafter, *Erläuterungen.* English translation: *Elucidations of Hölderlin's Poetry,* trans. Keith Hoeller (Amherst, N.Y.: Humanity Books, 2000), 48; hereafter, *Elucidations* (translation modified; Heidegger's emphasis).

4. In "Andenken," *Erläuterungen,* 150; "Remembrance," *Elucidations,* 170.

It is quite surprising to note that the translator of the *Elucidations* says nothing at all (in the introduction or notes) about the fundamental place of such painfully embarrassing statements, of which there are quite a few, or indeed of the overtly political project that is explicitly pursued in these readings. There is much to indicate that Heidegger's reading of Hölderlin is not first of all a matter of poetry—and that is one of Lacoue-Labarthe's grievances here.

Another word about this translation: While the renderings of Heidegger's essays and of the poems by Hölderlin included in it are quite faithful and even readable (no small feat when it comes to Heidegger), the reader of the present book will be frustrated in turning to the English *Elucidations* in search of some of the major terms invoked by Lacoue-Labarthe. One important example is *das Gedichtete,* "the poetized" or (as Lacoue-Labarthe prefers) "the *dictamen*" (see below, especially "*Il faut*" and "The Courage of Poetry"). This term is not translated in any consistent way in the *Elucidations,* but rather is dispersed into various circumlocutions, such as "what is composed in the poem."

5. See Lacoue-Labarthe, *La fiction du politique* (Paris: Christian Bourgois, 1987), translated as *Heidegger, Art, and Politics: The Fiction of the Political,* trans. Chris Turner (Oxford, U.K.: Blackwell, 1990). Hereafter cited as *Heidegger, Art, and Politics.* This book, which first appeared in 1987, was written before the so-called "Heidegger affair" took shape around the publication in France of Victor Farías's *Heidegger et le nazisme* (Lagrasse, Fr.: Verdier, 1987).

6. *Heidegger, Art, and Politics,* 2.

7. Lacoue-Labarthe has discussed this biographical myth, and Heidegger's resistance to it, in his Introduction to a selection of Hölderlin's poems in French translation entitled *Hymnes, élégies et autres poèmes* (Paris: Flammarion, 1983), 5–20.

8. In addition to *Heidegger, Art, and Politics,* see "The Nazi Myth" (co-written with Jean-Luc Nancy), trans. Brian Holmes, *Critical Inquiry* 16, 2 (Winter 1990): 291–312.

9. Paul de Man, "Heidegger's Exegeses of Hölderlin" (1955), in *Blindness and Insight* (Minneapolis: University of Minnesota Press, 1983), 250.

10. On this question, see especially Lacoue-Labarthe, "Hölderlin and the Greeks" and "The Caesura of the Speculative," in *Typography,* ed. Christopher Fynsk (Cambridge, Mass.: Harvard University Press, 1989).

11. Introduction, *Hymnes, élégies et autres poèmes,* 11–12.

12. See Maurice Blanchot, "Hölderlin's Itinerary" in *The Space of Literature,* trans. Ann Smock (Lincoln: University of Nebraska Press, 1982), 269–76.

13. Lacoue-Labarthe, *Poetry as Experience,* trans. Andrea Tarnowski (Stanford, Calif.: Stanford University Press, 1999); see especially "Two Poems by Paul Celan," 1–38.

14. "Entretien sur Hölderlin," *Détours d'écriture,* special issue on Hölderlin (April 1987): 119 (emphasis in the original).

15. Lacoue-Labarthe, *Phrase* (Paris: Christian Bourgois, 2000).

16. I am quoting (with minor modifications) from a translation of this poem by Leslie Hill, "Phrase VII," published in *On Jean-Luc Nancy: The Sense of*

Philosophy, eds. Darren Sheppard, Simon Sparks, and Colin Thomas (London: Routledge, 1997). The poem is dedicated to Nancy, who also taught at Berkeley around the same period.

Author's Preface

1. See *Heidegger, Art, and Politics.*

2. Lacoue-Labarthe has translated Hölderlin's versions of *Oedipus* and *Antigone* into French (together with the "Remarks" Hölderlin appended to his translations) and has collaborated on theatrical productions of these re-translations. See Hölderlin, *Antigone de Sophocle* (Paris: Christian Bourgois, 1978; 1998) and *Oedipe le tyran, de Sophocle* (Paris: Christian Bourgois, 1998).

3. On George, see Heidegger, "Das Wort," in *Unterwegs zur Sprache,* 10th ed. (Stuttgart: Neske, 1993), 219–38. English translation: "Words," in *On the Way to Language,* trans. Joan Stambaugh (San Francisco: Harper and Row, 1971), 139–56. On Trakl, see "Die Sprache im Gedicht," in *Unterwegs zur Sprache,* 35–82. English translation: "Language in the Poem," in *On the Way to Language,* trans. Peter D. Hertz, 159–98; and Jacques Derrida, *Of Spirit: Heidegger and the Question,* trans. Geoffrey Bennington and Rachel Bowlby (Chicago: University of Chicago Press, 1989), chap. 9 (83–98), and *"Geschlecht* 2: Heidegger's Hand," trans. John P. Leavey Jr., in *Deconstruction and Philosophy: The Texts of Jacques Derrida,* ed. John Sallis (Chicago: University of Chicago Press, 1987), 161–96.

4. Lacoue-Labarthe is referring to a short text by Heidegger, written at the insistence of René Char, commenting on certain phrases from Arthur Rimbaud's well-known "lettre du voyant." This text is published under the title "Rimbaud vivant" in *Aus der Erfahrung des Denkens, Gesamtausgabe,* vol. 13 (Frankfurt am Main: Klostermann, 1983), 225–27.

Prologue: Heidegger's Onto-Mythology

An earlier version of this text was presented at the *Romantik Symposium* held at the University of Tokyo in October 1998.

1. Heidegger, *Einführung in die Metaphysik,* 5th ed. (Tübingen: Max Niemeyer, 1987), 118. Hereafter cited as *Einführung.* English translation: *Introduction to Metaphysics,* trans. Gregory Fried and Richard Polt (New Haven, Conn.: Yale University Press, 2000), 164 (Heidegger's emphasis). Hereafter cited as *Introduction.*

2. *Einführung,* 118–19; *Introduction,* 165.

3. *Einführung,* 119; *Introduction,* 165.

4. *Einführung,* 119; *Introduction,* 166.

5. See in particular Lacoue-Labarthe, *L'imitation des modernes* (Paris: Galilée, 1986); *Heidegger, Art, and Politics;* and, with Jean-Luc Nancy, "Nazi Myth."

6. Author's note: But in fact it would be necessary to go back to the initial conditions leading to the collapse of Christianity in its Western, imperial, and Roman forms—that is, to the Reformation, or even the Renaissance, and to the first modern states created from national, and particularly linguistic, formations.

7. See Heidegger, "Was ist Metaphysik?" in *Wegmarken,* 3d ed. (Frankfurt am Main: Klostermann, 1996), 103–22; hereafter cited as *Wegmarken.* English translation: "What Is Metaphysics?" in *Pathmarks,* ed. William McNeill (Cambridge, U.K.: Cambridge University Press, 1998), 82–96; hereafter cited as *Pathmarks.*

8. Heidegger, "The Self-Assertion of the German University," trans. William S. Lewis, in *The Heidegger Controversy,* 2d ed., ed. Richard Wolin (Cambridge, Mass.: MIT Press, 1993), 29.

9. Interpolation introduced by Heidegger's translator in "Self-Assertion."

10. "Self-Assertion," 31.

11. *Ibid.,* 32.

12. *Hölderlins Hymnen "Germania" und "Der Rhein," Gesamtausgabe,* vol. 39 (Frankfurt am Main: Klostermann, 1980). Hereafter, *Hölderlins Hymnen.*

13. Author's note: It is well known that these variations on the derivatives of *springen* (jump, leap forth) trace out something like the harmonic network of the word *Ursprung:* the "origin" that gives the title—and the support—to the fundamental interrogation of these lectures.

14. Heidegger, "Der Ursprung des Kunstwerkes," in *Holzwege,* 6th ed. (Frankfurt am Main: Klostermann, 1980), 62; hereafter "Ursprung." English translation: "The Origin of the Work of Art," in *Off the Beaten Track,* eds. and trans. Julian Young and Kenneth Haynes (Cambridge, U.K.: Cambridge University Press, 2002), 48; hereafter "Origin."

Author's note: *Das Ungeheure,* a doublet of *das Unheimliche,* is the term that Hölderlin uses to translate *deinon* in Sophocles, and Heidegger himself will use it to render *daimon* in the well-known fragment from Heraclitus: *Ethos anthropo daimon* (see "Brief über den 'Humanismus,'" in *Wegmarken,* 354; English: "Letter on 'Humanism,'" in *Pathmarks,* 269).

15. Author's note: "als stiftende Bewahrung." Here Heidegger is playing on the root *wahr* (*wardon, Sanskrit —vara—, French "gare," English "ward") found also in *warten* (to wait), *Wartung* (maintenance) (compare the French "garder," "garde," English "guard"), as well as in *Wahrheit* ("truth") and many other derivatives (*bewahren,* to guard, to preserve; *wahrnehmen,* to perceive;

verwahren, to guarantee, to safeguard; *bergen,* to harbor, to shelter, to conceal [French *héberger*]; *die Wahrsage,* divination; *die Wahrnis,* protection, etc.). Among other passages, one can refer to "Anaximander's Saying" (also in *Off the Beaten Track,* particularly 262). In the lectures titled "The Origin of the Work of Art" from 1936, the term "guardians" (or "preservers") is used to designate that people which historically preserves the initial works of its destiny and is to be understood on the basis of this sort of "etymologism," which has resonances that are directly political *and* religious.

16. Heidegger, "Ursprung," 63–64; "Origin," 49.

17. Author's note: I will limit myself to citing the following, this time out of stupefaction (it is from the 1935 version of the lecture): "The beginning already contains the end, but in withdrawal. However, the beginning never has the inchoate character of the 'primitive' [*des "Primitiven"*]. The primitive, because it lacks the free leap [*Sprung*] and the intimate leaping-forth [*Vorsprung*], is always without a future. It is incapable of liberating anything else from out of itself, because it contains nothing other than what holds it captive. The beginning, on the contrary, is never primitive, that is, without an origin [*ursprungslos*], but is indeed initiatory: It is what is not-yet-closed. The apparent awkwardness, crudeness, and even indigence that can be associated with it are only the strangeness of this firmness that comes to face a closed plenitude. Whenever a beginning prepares to make the leap, it always has the appearance of a relapse. For precisely the beginning is unable to lead the familiar back onto the sure and well-known path it has followed up to then. The traditional remains in place, but it is out of joint. Confusion and loss prevail. [Let us not forget that this was written in 1935 and that it is not merely a reference to the age of Pericles.—L.-L.] That is a consequence of the growing powerlessness of the ordinary—not of the beginning itself. For the beginning has a deeper foundation, which is why it must dig beneath the foundation that was previously laid. Hence the ambiguity, which can last for a long time, about whether the inevitable semblance of a relapse will lead in fact to a rising or a setting." *De l'origine de l'oeuvre d'art,* ed. and trans. E. Martineau (n.p.: Authentica, 1987).

18. Heidegger, "Ursprung," 59; "Origin," 46.

19. Heidegger, "Ursprung," 60; "Origin," 46. The last two interpolations are mine (Trans.).

20. "Die Fabel, poetische Ansicht der Geschichte, und Architektonik des Himmels beschäftigt mich gegenwärtig vorzüglich, besonders das Nationelle, sofern es von dem Griechischen verschieden ist." Letter to Leo von Seckendorf, 12 March 1804. *Sämtliche Werke,* "Grosse Stuttgarter Ausgabe," eds. Friedrich

Beissner and Adolf Beck (Stuttgart: Kohlhammer, 1946–85), vol. 6: 1, 437. Hereafter cited as *GSA*, followed by the volume and page numbers.

21. My interpolations; I have followed the French translation cited by Lacoue-Labarthe in rendering *Sagen* as "saying" and *Sage* as "fable."

22. "Ursprung," 60; "Origin," 46.

23. See "Typography," in *Typography: Mimesis, Philosophy, Politics*, ed. Christopher Fynsk (Stanford, Calif.: Stanford University Press, 1998), 43–138.

24. "Ursprung," 28–29; "Origin," 22.

25. "Ursprung," 30; "Origin," 23.

26. Author's note: It is not difficult to see here one of the many variations on the analysis of the Aristotelian *logos apophantikos* in section 7 of *Being and Time*.

27. This is the case in the German edition and the French translation; the English translation changes the order of the essays; see the following note.

28. Heidegger, "Der Weg zur Sprache" in *Unterwegs zur Sprache*, 10th ed. (Stuttgart: Günther Neske, 1993), 253. English translation: "The Way to Language," in *On the Way to Language*, trans. Peter D. Hertz (San Francisco: Harper and Row, 1971), 123.

29. Heidegger, *Einführung*, 131; *Introduction*, 182–83.

Chapter 1: Poetry, Philosophy, Politics

This lecture was first presented at the University of California at Irvine in 1987; it was reworked in 1988 and presented at the University of Geneva, then in 1990, for a seminar organized by Jacques Rancière at the Collège international de philosophie; the proceedings of this conference were edited by Rancière and published under the title *La Politique des poètes: Pourquoi des poètes en temps de détresse* (Paris: Albin Michel, 1992). A few emendations have been added here.

1. Badiou, *Manifeste pour la philosophie* (Paris: Seuil, 1989) (cited hereafter as *Manifeste*). English translation: *Manifesto for Philosophy*, trans. Norman Madarasz (Albany, N.Y.: SUNY Press, 1999) (cited hereafter, with many modifications, as *Manifesto*). *L'Être et l'événement* (Paris: Seuil, 1988) has recently appeared in an English translation as *Being and Event*, trans. Oliver Feltham (London: Continuum, 2005).

2. See Jacques Rancière, ed., *La Politique des poètes: Pourquoi des poètes en temps de détresse* (Paris: Albin Michel, 1992).

3. *Manifeste*, 58; *Manifesto*, 77.

4. *Manifeste,* 68; *Manifesto,* 86.

5. *Manifeste,* 57; *Manifesto,* 76.

6. *Manifeste,* 54–55; *Manifesto,* 73–74.

7. *Manifeste,* 54; *Manifesto,* 74.

8. *Manifeste,* 68–69; *Manifesto,* 87.

9. Plato, *Laws,* VII, 817b.

10. It is under this title that Fichte's *Wissenschaftslehre* has been translated into English. See *The Science of Knowledge,* trans. Peter Heath and John Lachs (Cambridge, U.K.: Cambridge University Press, 1982).

11. My interpolation; the French translation cited by Lacoue-Labarthe gives the term *génération,* which he refers to below. See also "Epilogue: The Spirit of National Socialism and Its Destiny," in this volume.

12. Friedrich Wilhelm Joseph von Schelling, *System of Transcendental Idealism (1800),* trans. Peter Heath (Charlottesville: University Press of Virginia, 1978), 232–33.

13. Lacoue-Labarthe is referring to a brief text of uncertain authorship entitled "The Oldest System-Program of German Idealism." This text is translated and given a lengthy commentary in Lacoue-Labarthe and Nancy, *L'Absolu littéraire* (Paris: Seuil, 1978), 39–54; for an English translation of this commentary, see *The Literary Absolute,* trans. Philippe Bernard and Cheryl Lester (Albany, N.Y.: SUNY Press, 1988), 27–37; for a translation of the "Oldest System-Program," see Hölderlin, *Essays and Letters on Theory,* trans. Thomas Pfau (Albany, N.Y.: SUNY Press, 1988), 154–56.

14. Schelling, *The Philosophy of Art,* trans. Douglass Stott (Minneapolis: University of Minnesota Press, 1989), 280. (The translator there uses the expression "worship service" for "Mass.")

15. On these points, see Lacoue-Labarthe, *Musica Ficta (Figures of Wagner),* trans. Felicia McCarren (Stanford, Calif.: Stanford University Press, 1994).

16. See *Heidegger, Art, and Politics,* ch. 6, esp. 53.

17. See "Two Poems by Paul Celan," in *Poetry as Experience,* trans. Andrea Tarnowski (Stanford, Calif.: Stanford University Press, 1999), 1–38.

18. *Wegmarken,* 338–39; *Pathmarks,* 257–58.

19. *Wegmarken,* 337–38; *Pathmarks,* 257.

20. Letter of June 1917 (Benjamin's emphasis), in *The Correspondence of Walter Benjamin, 1910–1940,* eds. Gerschom Scholem and Theodor Adorno, trans. Manfred R. Jacobson and Evelyn M. Jacobson (Chicago: University of Chicago Press, 1994), 88.

21. Benjamin, "Der Begriff der Kunstkritik in der deutschen Romantik," in

Gesammelte Schriften 1: 1, 103. English translation: "The Concept of Criticism in German Romanticism," trans. D. Lachterman, H. Eiland, and I. Balfour, in *Selected Writings,* vol. 1, 175.

22. Hölderlin, quoted in Benjamin, *Gesammelte Schriften,* 1: 1, 105; *Selected Writings,* 1, 176.

23. "O mathématiques sévères . . ." Cited in *Manifeste,* 56; *Manifesto,* 75. See Isidore Lucien Ducasse, comte de Lautréamont, *Les Chants de Maldoror,* 2: 10; *Songs of Maldoror,* trans. Paul Knight (London: Penguin, 1978).

24. *Manifeste,* 84; *Manifesto,* 101.

Chapter 2: *Il faut*

Lecture presented in 1991 as part of the *Turm-Vorträge* organized by the Hölderlin-Gesellschaft in Tübingen. A first version was published in French in the United States in *MLN* 107 (1992): 421–40; the text was later reworked, partly at the request of Valérie Lawitschka, editor of the *Turm-Vorträge.* This lecture was already dedicated to Roger Laporte when it was first presented.

1. See Blanchot, *The Infinite Conversation,* trans. Susan Hanson (Minneapolis: University of Minnesota Press, 1993), xii (translation modified).

2. Despite its awkwardness in translation, and because it will be a question here of very specific idiomatic expressions, I will retain Lacoue-Labarthe's references to his own language.

3. This idiom is indeed irreplaceable. An explanatory remark may be useful here: The expression *il faut* is based on the verb *falloir* (to be necessary), but it is used only in the third person, where "il" is not a personal pronoun but an impersonal "it"; because of the verbal structure of the utterance (unlike the English "it is necessary"), this "it" almost seems to indicate the (active) source of a command. Hence its categorical force, particularly when the infinitive that often follows it (it is necessary to . . .) remains unspecified, rendering the command "intransitive."

4. Here too a note of explanation may be helpful: *Faillir* cannot be given a simple equivalent; it is used mainly in past tense, compound expressions meaning "to have almost" done such and such. In a sense it means "to fail" but is very often used for acts or events that one was not intending to bring about, for example "j'ai failli tomber": I almost fell. "Faillir" is thus linked, etymologically and semantically, to a loss of power or will, to that which is beyond the sphere of intention. (It is interesting to note that in the American South a similar locution is still used in English; for example, the exclamation

"I like to have died!" means that, for whatever sudden and unexpected reason, I almost died, I "lacked" very little before doing so.)

5. These quotations are all found at the end of the "Remarks on Oedipus" that Hölderlin appended to his translation of Sophocles. See "Anmerkungen zum Oedipus" in *GSA* 5, 201–2. For an English translation, see Friedrich Hölderlin, *Essays and Letters on Theory,* ed. T. Pfau (Albany, N.Y.: SUNY Press, 1988).

6. See *Manifesto for Philosophy.*

7. Todtnauberg was the location of Heidegger's cabin in the Black Forest; Celan used the name as the title of a poem written after his visit.

8. Adorno is quoting from *Erläuterungen,* 107–8; *Elucidations,* 130–31.

9. Adorno, "Parataxis. Zur späten Lyrik Hölderlins," in *Noten zur Literatur* (Frankfurt am Main: Suhrkamp, 1974), 457–58; hereafter cited as *Noten.* English translation: "Parataxis. On Hölderlin's Late Poetry," in *Notes to Literature,* vol. 2, trans. S. Weber Nicholson (New York: Columbia University Press, 1992), 118; hereafter cited as *Notes.* This translation will be cited with minor modifications when necessary.

10. Walter Benjamin, *Deutsche Menschen. Eine Folge von Briefen* (Frankfurt am Main: Suhrkamp, 1962), 41. The phrase is cited by Adorno, who writes: "Hölderlin's intentionless language, the 'naked rock' of which is 'everywhere exposed,' is an ideal, that of revealed language" (*Noten,* 478; *Notes* 2, 137).

11. Author's note: See Jean-Pierre Lefebvre, "Auch die Stege sind Holzwege" in *Hölderlin vue de France,* ed. Bernhard Böschenstein and Jacque Le Rider (Tübingen: Gunther Narr Verlag, 1987). See also "Neue Fragestellungen zu Hölderlins Reisen und zu seinem Aufenthalt in Frankreich," Hölderlin Gesellschaft, *Turm-Vorträge 1987/88,* ed. Valérie Lawitschka (Tübingen: n.p., 1988). And Jean-Pierre Lefebvre, *Hölderlin, journal de Bordeaux* (Bordeaux: William Blake, 1990).

12. *Das Gedichtete* has often been translated as "the poetized," which will be used here except where Lacoue-Labarthe uses *le dictamen*; this will be given literally as "the *dictamen.*" See page 51 and note 36 below.

13. Lacoue-Labarthe is of course referring to French translations of the poem; the one he cites is by Jean-Pierre Lefebvre. The English translation given here is by Michael Hamburger (Hölderlin, *Selected Verse* [Baltimore: Penguin, 1961], 209–10), which I modify slightly (Hamburger's "plain prose translations" in this bilingual edition omit all line breaks).

14. *Noten,* 458; *Notes* 2, 118–19.

15. *Noten,* 456; *Notes* 2, 117.

16. *The Jargon of Authenticity*, trans. Knut Tarnowski and Frederic Will (Evanston, Ill.: Northwestern University Press, 1973).

17. Hölderlin, *GSA* 6: 1, 426; *Essays and Letters on Theory*, 150.

18. In French: *é-loignement*. Heidegger's (often hyphenated) use of the common German word *Entfernung*, whose prefix oscillates between an intensifier and a negation, has been translated variously as "dis-distance," "de-distance," and "deseverance." The choice used here attempts to play on a similarly common word in English.

19. See "The Caesura of the Speculative" in *Typography: Mimesis, Philosophy, Politics*, ed. Christopher Fynsk (Stanford, Calif.: Stanford University Press, 1998), esp. 231.

20. *Noten*, 458; *Notes* 2, 119. The lines from Hölderlin are from the poem that begins "Einst hab ich die Muse gefragt" ("Once I asked the Muse").

21. *Noten*, 452; *Notes* 2, 114.

22. *Noten*, 451; *Notes* 2, 112.

23. *Noten*, 455–56; *Notes* 2, 116–17. The lines from Hölderlin are from "Die Wanderung" ("The Journey").

24. *Erläuterungen*, 90, note; *Elucidations*, 173, note 2.

25. *Noten*, 460; *Notes* 2, 120–21.

26. *Noten*, 460–61; *Notes* 2, 121.

27. *Noten*, 462; *Notes* 2, 122.

28. *Noten*, 459; *Notes* 2, 120.

29. *Erläuterungen*, 41; *Elucidations*, 59.

30. *Noten*, 462; *Notes* 2, 122.

31. *Noten*, 462; *Notes* 2, 122.

32. *Noten*, 461; *Notes* 2, 121.

33. In French: *retour amont*. This is the title of a collection of poetry published by René Char in 1966.

34. "Zwei Gedichte von Friedrich Hölderlin," in *Gesammelte Schriften*, eds. Rolf Tiedemann and Hermann Schweppenhauser (Frankfurt am Main: Suhrkamp, 1977), 2: 1, 105–26; hereafter cited as *Schriften* 2: 1. English translation: "Two Poems by Friedrich Hölderlin," trans. S. Corngold, in Walter Benjamin, *Selected Writings*, vol. 1, eds. M. Bullock and M. Jennings (Cambridge, Mass.: Harvard University Press, 1996), 18–36; hereafter cited as *Writings* 1.

35. Adorno, *Aesthetic Theory*, tr. R. Hullot-Kentor (Minneapolis: University of Minnesota Press, 1997).

36. *Dictare* is Latin for "to dictate" and is related etymologically to the German word *dichten*, to write poetry or "to poetize." See "The Courage of Poetry," chap. 3 in this volume.

37. Thomas Mann, "Freud and the Future" in *Essays of Three Decades* (New York: Knopf, 1947).

38. At this point Lacoue-Labarthe interrupts the quotation of the published French translation to make the following remark: "The French translation here is very rough: Benjamin says more precisely that the mythic connections are given form from a figure (*Gestalt*) that it is impossible to conceive in a more precise way—and the very heavy philosophical weight carried by this word is well known." On this last point, see Lacoue-Labarthe's essay "Typography," in *Typography: Mimesis, Philosophy, Politics,* 43–138.

39. Benjamin, *Schriften* 2: 1, 126; *Writings* 1, 35–36. The lines from Hölderlin are from the poem "Der Herbst" ("Autumn").

40. The word *heilignüchtern* (sacredly sober) is found in "Hälfte des Lebens" ("The Middle of Life").

41. Benjamin, *Schriften* 2: 1, 125–26; *Writings* 1, 35.

42. Hölderlin, *GSA* 6: 1, 426; *Essays and Letters on Theory,* 150.

43. *Noten,* 471; *Notes* 2, 130.

44. Adorno, "Music and Language: A Fragment," in *Quasi una Fantasia: Essays on Modern Music,* trans. Rodney Livingstone (London: Verso Books, 1998), 2.

45. *Noten,* 471; *Notes* 2, 130.

46. *Noten,* 463; *Notes* 2, 123.

47. Charles Baudelaire, "The Swan," in *Flowers of Evil.*

48. A generic term of respect, designating high birth and nobility (and meaning literally "beautiful-and-good"), used as an epithet for aristocratic Greeks.

49. Parting, leave-taking, farewell.

50. *Daselbst* has in German the flat and impersonal overtones of its closest English equivalent, "thereat."

51. *Erläuterungen,* 108; *Elucidations,* 131.

52. Benjamin, "Der Begriff der Kunstkritik in der deutschen Romantik," in *Schriften* 1: 1, 103. English translation: "The Concept of Criticism in German Romanticism," trans. D. Lachterman, H. Eiland, and I. Balfour, in *Writings,* vol. 1, 175.

53. *Schriften* 1: 1, 175–76; *Writings* 1, 508–9.

Chapter 3: The Courage of Poetry

This lecture was presented on June 23, 1993, at the Maison des Écrivains de Paris as part of the *Conférences du Perroquet,* at the invitation of Alain Badiou. It was announced in the program by the following note:

When philosophy addresses itself to poetry, it takes on a responsibility—and, moreover, it claims this responsibility as its own: It responds, it says, to the responsibility with which poetry itself believes itself to be authorized.

Heidegger, a notable example, responds to Hölderlin in order to respond for him. It is a matter, he thinks, of courage as such, which is the courage of History.

This project, as I will attempt to show, is theologico-political. It is a formidable project, in that it tries to deepen and insists on *verifying* fascism. I would like to make an incision here, in a mode that would not be simply in opposition, with a theologico-poetic project. This is Benjamin's project: It would have the immense merit of recognizing the theological in the figure of its failure, and of turning poetry—whence we came—toward prose, where we are.

A first version of this text was published in *Conférences du Perroquet* 39 (June 1993).

1. *Hölderlins Hymnen*, 213–14.

2. "Hölderlin et l'essence de la poésie," in Martin Heidegger, *Qu'est-ce que la métaphysique?* (Paris: Gallimard, 1938).

3. *Hölderlins Hymnen*, 1.

4. "Spiegel-Gespräch, mit Martin Heidegger," in *Antwort: Martin Heidegger im Gespräch,* eds. Günther Neske and Emil Kettering (Pfullingen, Ger.: Neske, 1988), 99–100; "'Only a God Can Save Us': *Der Spiegel*'s Interview with Martin Heidegger (1966)" in *The Heidegger Controversy,* ed. Richard Wolin (Cambridge, Mass.: MIT Press, 1993), 107.

5. *Wegmarken*, 338–39; *Pathmarks*, 257–58.

6. *Wegmarken*, 338; *Pathmarks*, 257.

7. Author's note: In a remarkable recent study, entitled "Un peuple métaphysique" (*Revue de métaphysique et de morale, "Philosophies nationales? Controverses franco-allemandes"* [Paris, PUF, September 2001]), Jean-François Courtine sees this "monstrous" formula as a "pseudo-citation" of Mme. de Staël (*De l'Allemagne,* III, 7), who used it in a way that was at least tinged with doubt, if not altogether ironic.

8. See Lacoue-Labarthe and Nancy, "Nazi Myth"; and Epilogue: "The Spirit of National Socialism and Its Destiny," in this volume.

9. See "Poetry, Philosophy, Politics," chap. 1, in this volume.

10. *Erläuterungen*, 36–37; *Elucidations*, 55.

11. *Erläuterungen*, 37; *Elucidations*, 55.

12. Benjamin, "Zwei Gedichte von Friedrich Hölderlin," in *Schriften,* 2: 1, 105–26; "Two Poems by Friedrich Hölderlin," trans. S. Corngold, in *Writings,* vol. 1, 18–36.

13. The English translator of Benjamin's essay chooses "Timidity."

14. The translator of the French version of Benjamin's essay to which Lacoue-Labarthe refers. See "Deux poèmes de Friedrich Hölderlin," in Benjamin, *Mythe et violence* (Paris: Denoël, 1971), 51–78.

15. The French term Lacoue-Labarthe refers to here is *le poématique.* The English translator of Benjamin's essay chooses "the poetized." Following Lacoue-Labarthe's usage, I will use "the *dictamen.*"

16. Quoted in *Schriften,* 2: 1, 105; *Writings* 1, 19.

17. "Goethes Wahlverwandtschaften," in *Schriften* 1: 1, 125; "Goethe's Elective Affinities," trans. Stanley Corngold, in *Writings* 1, 297.

18. *Schriften* 2: 1, 105; *Writings* 1, 18; translator's interpolations. "Intuitive" in this context has the Kantian sense of sensory receptivity; Corngold translates it as "perceptual."

19. *Erläuterungen,* 36; *Elucidations,* 54.

20. *Marturos* is the Greek word for "witness."

21. *Schriften* 2: 1, 105–6; *Writings* 1, 18–19.

22. Immanuel Kant, *Critique of Pure Reason,* A141; B181.

23. *Schriften* 2: 1, 106–7; *Writings* 1, 19–20.

24. "Dichterisch"; "Poetically."

25. Thomas Mann, "Freud and the Future," in *Essays of Three Decades* (New York: Knopf, 1947).

26. *Schriften* 2: 1, 107; *Writings* 1, 20.

27. *Schriften* 2: 1, 108; *Writings* 1, 20–21.

28. *Schriften* 2: 1, 109–10; *Writings* 1, 22–23.

29. *Schriften* 2: 1, 114; *Writings* 1, 26 (Corngold gives: "conversion of the mythological.")

30. See Adorno, "Parataxis. Zur späten Lyrik Hölderlins" in *Noten zur Literatur* (Frankfurt am Main: Suhrkamp, 1974), 455. English translation: "Parataxis. On Hölderlin's Late Poetry" in *Notes to Literature,* vol. 2, trans. S. Weber Nicholson (New York: Columbia University Press, 1992), 116.

31. *Schriften* 2: 1, 124; *Writings* 1, 33–34.

32. *Schriften* 2: 1, 124–25; *Writings* 1, 34.

33. *Schriften* 2: 1, 125–26; *Writings* 1, 35.

34. *Schriften* 2: 1, 126; *Writings* 1, 35–36.

35. Benjamin, *Der Begriff der Kunstkritik in der deutschen Romantik,* in *Schriften* 1: 1, 100–101; *The Concept of Criticism in German Romanticism,* in *Writings* 1, 173.

36. See Lacoue-Labarthe, "De l'éthique: à propos d'Antigone" in *Lacan avec les philosophes,* ed. Collège international de philosophie (Paris: Albin Michel, 1991), 19–36.

Epilogue: The Spirit of National Socialism and Its Destiny

Lecture presented on May 12, 1995, in Freiburg im Breisgau, Germany, at the colloquium "Postmoderne und Fundamentalismus—Neue semantische und politische Frontstellungen," organized as part of the "Freiburger Kulturgespräch im Marienbad." Michael Hirsch of the Institut für Soziale Gegenwartsfragen, co-organizer of the colloquium, specifically asked me to bring together some of the arguments from my work on Heidegger (especially *Heidegger, Art, and Politics*). He also provided an improvised translation of my lecture as I presented it, for which I would like to thank him here. The present version, with a few modifications, was published in *Cahiers philosophiques de Strasbourg* 5 (1997).

1. For the "amended" version of Heidegger's remarks, published many years later, see *Einführung*, 152; *Introduction*, 213.

2. Lacoue-Labarthe writes "dans tout retrait se retrace ce dont on se retire."

3. See "Brief über den 'Humanismus,'" in *Wegmarken*, 313–64; "Letter on 'Humanism,'" in *Pathmarks*, 239–76.

4. See *Einführung*, 117; *Introduction*, 162–63.

5. Ernst Kantorowicz, *The King's Two Bodies: A Study in Mediaeval Political Theology* (Princeton, N.J.: Princeton University Press, 1981), esp. 242.

6. "Ursprung," 48; "Origin," 37.

7. *Einführung*, 152; *Introduction*, 213.

8. See Lacoue-Labarthe, *Heidegger, Art, and Politics*, trans. Chris Turner (London: Basil Blackwell, 1990).

9. Heidegger, "Zur Seinsfrage," in *Wegmarken*, 385–426; "On the Question of Being," in *Pathmarks*, 291–322.

10. See Jacques Derrida, "*Geschlecht* 2: Heidegger's Hand," trans. John P. Leavey Jr., in *Deconstruction and Philosophy: The Texts of Jacques Derrida*, ed. John Sallis (Chicago: University of Chicago Press, 1987), 161–96.

11. Author's note: Allow me to refer here to the analyses that Jean-Luc Nancy and I developed in "The Nazi Myth."

12. See Heidegger, *Being and Time*, section 74.

13. See Heidegger, "The Self-Assertion of the German University," trans. William S. Lewis in *The Heidegger Controversy*, 2d ed., ed. Richard Wolin (Cambridge, Mass.: MIT Press, 1993), 29–39.

14. *Hölderlins Hymnen*, 214.

15. See Domenico Losurdo, "Heidegger and Hitler's War," in *The Heidegger Case: On Philosophy and Politics,* eds. Tom Rockmore and Joseph Margolis (Philadelphia: Temple University Press, 1992), 141–64 (esp. 141).

16. Author's note: Quoted by Arno Münster, *Nietzsche et le nazisme* (Paris: L'Harmattan, 1995).

17. This word evokes the disorientation of "not being at home" or in one's own country (*pays*); it is similar to the *Heimatlosigkeit* (homelessness) evoked above, but corresponds even more closely to the German word *Unheimlichkeit* (discussed by Heidegger on a number of occasions, particularly in *Being and Time,* section 40, and often taken up by Lacoue-Labarthe), usually translated as "uncanniness." In this context it also evokes the migration from the country to the city.

18. Quoted in Botho Strauss, "Anschwellender Bocksgesang," in *Die Selbstbewusste Nation,* eds. Heimo Schwilk and Ulrich Schocht (Berlin: Ullstein, 1994), 39.

Index of Personal Names

PHILIPPE LACOUE-LABARTHE is a professor emeritus of philosophy and aesthetics at the University of Strasbourg. He is the author of several books previously translated into English: *Typography, The Subject of Philosophy, The Literary Absolute* (with Jean-Luc Nancy), *Musica Ficta,* and *Poetry as Experience.*

JEFF FORT is an assistant professor of French at the University of California, Davis. His previous translations include Maurice Blanchot's *Aminadab,* Jean Genet's *Declared Enemy,* Jacques Derrida and Elisabeth Roudinesco's *For What Tomorrow . . . ,* and Jean-Luc Nancy's *Ground of the Image.*

The University of Illinois Press
is a founding member of the
Association of American University Presses.

Composed in 10.5/13 Adobe Minion
at the University of Illinois Press
Designed by Dennis Roberts
Manufactured by Thomson-Shore, Inc.

University of Illinois Press
1325 South Oak Street
Champaign, IL 61820-6903
www.press.uillinois.edu